SECOND EDITION

LEADERSHIP AND

MAKING
VISIONS **FUTURING**
HAPPEN

SECOND EDITION

LEADERSHIP AND

MAKING
VISIONS
HAPPEN
FUTURING

JOHN R. HOYLE

Foreword by Edward Cornish
Founder and Former President
The World Future Society

CORWIN PRESS
A SAGE Publications Company
Thousand Oaks, California

For information:

Corwin Press
A Sage Publications Company
2455 Teller Road
Thousand Oaks, California 91320
www.corwinpress.com

Sage Publications Ltd.
1 Oliver's Yard
55 City Road
London EC1Y 1SP
United Kingdom

Sage Publications India Pvt. Ltd.
B-42, Panchsheel Enclave
Post Box 4109
New Delhi 110 017 India

Printed in the United States of America.

Library of Congress Cataloging-in-Publication Data

Hoyle, John.
Leadership and futuring : making visions happen / John R. Hoyle.— 2nd ed.
    p. cm.
Includes bibliographical references and index.
ISBN 1-4129-3847-3 (cloth)—ISBN 1-4129-3848-1 (pbk.)
    1. Leadership. 2. Planning. I. Title.
HD57.7.H69 2007
658.4′092—dc22

                                                           2006004653

This book is printed on acid-free paper.

06   07   08   09   10   10   9   8   7   6   5   4   3   2   1

Acquisitions Editor:	Elizabeth Brenkus
Editorial Assistant:	Desirée Enayati
Production Editor:	Jenn Reese
Copy Editor:	Cate Huisman
Typesetter:	C&M Digitals (P) Ltd.
Proofreader:	William Stoddard
Indexer:	Ellen Slavitz

Contents

Foreword   vii

    By Edward Cornish

Acknowledgments   ix

About the Author   xi

Introduction   1

1. What's Leadership Got to Do With Futuring?   7

2. Visionary Leaders I Have Known and
   Others I Wish I Had Known   37

3. Motivating Others to Engage in Futuring   55

4. Making Visions Happen   65

5. Staff Development Techniques to Envision
   and Create Real-World Programs   75

6. The Visionary Leader You Can Become   99

Bibliography and References   111

Index   119

Foreword

Abraham Lincoln once said, "If we could first know where we are and whither we are tending, we could better judge what to do and how to do it."

Lincoln's advice applies especially to leaders and those aspiring to leadership. We cannot be a light for others if we ourselves are in darkness. Before leading others, we must understand the world around us and how it is changing. Only then can we reasonably judge what should be done and create visions that will inspire people to do it.

But let's not kid ourselves: It's extraordinarily difficult today to know "where we are and whither we are tending." Globalization means that we have to take account of events occurring in lands we never heard of, because they can cost us our jobs and even our lives. Furthermore, our world is experiencing the fastest technological and social change in history. The only useful way I know to keep up with what's happening in the world around us is by *futuring*. This term may be unfamiliar to you, but the activity—seriously trying to figure out what is likely to happen in the future—is something we all do when we have to plan for future events in our personal lives, such as giving a party, going on vacation, getting a new job, moving to another city, etc.

Most futuring is done intuitively by people trying to imagine what might happen in the future, but since World War II, scholars, scientists, and other futurists have refined some useful ways to monitor global changes and forecast future developments. These techniques include trend monitoring and analysis, the generation of scenarios, Delphi polling, and gaming. Furthermore, there is an expanding body of books and journals discussing current trends and where they may lead. In addition, the World Future Society (wfs.org) holds yearly conferences where futurists share their latest thinking about the future.

You can start right now to expand your knowledge of futuring as well as leadership by reading this excellent book, *Leadership and Futuring*. The author, Professor John R. Hoyle, is a thoroughly trustworthy guide who has spent many years in leadership training. In 2004, his peers honored him as an "Exceptional Living Scholar" in educational administration. Professor Hoyle provides a wealth of wise advice on leadership, and it's a pleasure to note that he also has a very engaging writing style. Readers will enjoy as well as learn from the many vivid anecdotes based on his personal experience.

But, in my view, what makes *Leadership and Futuring* a really important book for all who aspire to leadership is that it squarely confronts the extraordinary challenge that the current global transformation poses for leaders, and it suggests constructive ways to deal with it through futuring.

Edward Cornish
Editor, *The Futurist Magazine*
Founder, World Future Society
Bethesda, Maryland, February 2006

Acknowledgments

I wish to thank my students and colleagues for the many ideas that they have shared with me and that are on each page of this second edition. I owe much to Texas A&M University for the opportunities to teach, conduct research, and advise the best students in America. I thank all of you in public schools, universities, law enforcement, business, and religious organizations who have enriched my life over the past 30 years by inviting me to serve as your speaker and seminar leader around the world. I am deeply grateful to my English-instructor spouse Carolyn Hoyle, who edited each page and is my best friend—who loves to travel, serve as church board chair, advise students in Kappa Kappa Gamma sorority, plan family gatherings, attend our grandsons' football games, attend our granddaughter's dance and theater performances, and pull for our Aggie athletic teams (some seasons are more fun than others). Also, thanks to Bill Ashworth, my good friend, for assisting with the graphics and other details. Finally, I dedicate the book to the heroes found in Chapter 2 and to my outstanding counselor son John Jr., his best-ever science-teacher wife Julie, and their perfect children Winston and Jennifer of College Station. Also, this work is dedicated to the best teacher in Friendswood, Texas, our daughter Laura, and to Ross Sanders, the best son-in-law in the nation. The two of them produced two perfect grandsons: David, a student at Texas A&M, and Michael, a sophomore at Friendswood High School in Friendswood, Texas.

Corwin Press gratefully acknowledges the contributions of the following individuals:

Rosemarie Young, Principal
Watson Lane Elementary School
Louisville, KY
NAESP President

Bess Scott, Principal
McPhee Elementary School
Lincoln, NE

Brenda Dietrich, Superintendent
Auburn-Washburn Unified School District
Topeka, KS

Karen Tichy, Associate Superintendent for Instruction
Archdiocese of Saint Louis
St. Louis, MO

Nancy M. Moga, Principal
Callaghan Elementary School
Covington, VA

Donald Poplau, Principal
Mankato East Senior High School
Mankato, MN

Dan Lawson, Superintendent
Tullahoma City Schools
Tullahoma, TN

Gloria Kumagai, Principal
Museum Magnet Elementary School
St. Paul, MN

About the Author

 **John R. Hoyle** specializes in leadership preparation, research, and development and in future studies. In 2004 he was selected by his peers across the nation as one of four "Exceptional Living Scholars" in educational administration. The others are John Goodlad, Joseph Murphy, and Tom Sergiovanni. During his distinguished career in higher education, he has written, coauthored, or edited 10 books; produced over 130 articles and book chapters on administrator standards and preparation and on organizational and leadership studies; and presented over 300 keynote addresses and leadership seminars around the world. Hoyle's recent works include *Leadership and the Force of Love: Six Keys to Motivating With Love* (Corwin Press, 2002) and (as coauthor) *The Superintendent as CEO: Standards-Based Performance* (Corwin Press, 2005). One of his books, coauthored with Fenwick English and Betty Steffy and titled *Skills for Successful 21st Century School Leaders* (1998), continues to be one of the most widely used textbooks in the field of educational administration. Dr. Hoyle has been American Association of School Administrators (AASA) professor of the year, has served as president of the National Council of Professors of Educational Administration, and was chair of the National Commission on Standards for the Superintendency in 1993. These standards became the benchmark for later standards. In addition, Hoyle served as a member of the AASA advisory board on systems leadership and as the AASA representative on the advisory committee for the creation of standards for advanced programs in educational leadership for the National Council for the Accreditation of Colleges of Education. He has been labeled an educational futurist in interviews by *U.S. News and World Report, Omni Magazine,*

and *USA Today*. Dr. Hoyle is professor of educational administration at Texas A&M University, where he teaches classes in futurism and global change, organizational leadership and theory, and program evaluation. Hoyle holds two university awards for distinguished achievement in teaching. A popular keynote speaker and workshop consultant, he works with schools, universities, agricultural agencies, the California Command College for Law Enforcement, and businesses in the United States and abroad. He played first base on a conference champion Aggie baseball team and served seven years as a public school teacher, coach, and administrator. Hoyle has taught in five universities in the United States and also taught one year in Europe with Boston University. He holds a PhD in education and social science from Texas A&M University.

Introduction

C ome on now, admit it, wouldn't you like to be viewed by others as a visionary leader with the knowledge and skills to make things happen? Reading this book and applying the suggested skills for personal and team improvement may not suddenly make you a dynamic visionary, but if you add another layer of skills and motivation strategies, perhaps it can assist you in reaching your dream position and accomplishing great things in your personal life and career. Mike Vance, former dean of Disney University and author of *Think Out of the Box* (1995), and other creative thinkers realize that merely being worried about the future is not enough, and that merely staring into the future will reveal little creative thinking. We futurists constantly remind our students and other clients to "THINK OUT OF THE BOX!" Thinking out of the box is a metaphor for creative futuring. To practice it, try connecting the nine zeros below by drawing only four straight lines without lifting your pen.

0   0   0

0   0   0

0   0   0

Hint: THINK OUT OF THE BOX.

Thinking out of the box and other creative thinking activities are a good start toward unfreezing our minds to anticipate and manage our future world. This book will provide numerous exercises to lead your team to some breakthrough thinking about creating exciting, equitable, and high-performing schools, agencies, companies, and other organizations. According to Thomas Friedman (2005), "The world has gone from round to flat . . . and if I am right about the flattening of the world, it will be remembered as one of those fundamental changes—like the rise of the nation-state or the industrial revolution" (p. 45). Freidman's ten world flatteners include the removal of the Berlin Wall, which liberated millions from fear and communist domination toward the hope of democracy and free trade; Netscape, the Internet browser that brought the power of information to millions of people; outsourcing through the convenience of fiber optics and instant communications for marketing; and offshoring, which has saved U.S. consumers $600 billion and vastly improved the economies of India, China, and other nations around the world. The real anxiety of living in a flat world is whether the education system of the United States will prepare enough creative scientists, engineers, and school and corporate leaders to enable the country to keep its competitive edge. America must remain the leader in developing new technologies and total systems that other nations desire to duplicate. America needs futurists with the vision to inspire minds to create systems for better nutrition, housing, education, health care, travel, and political structures. Also, new visionaries are needed to help build a future where social justice is more than lofty words tossed about by social reformers and political hopefuls.

This book is about broadening your skills to create new and exciting learning organizations and, in the words of Henry Kissinger, to "take people [from] where they are and take them to places they have never been." Visionaries and their visions have inspired the creation of magnificent monuments that have withstood the ravages of time. The Greek temples, the Roman Colosseum, the chateaus of France, and Epcot Center had their genesis in someone's vision. According to leadership scholars Warren Bennis and Burt Nanus (1985), vision promotes a condition that is significantly better than the status quo by expressing a realistic, credible, and attractive organizational future. They speak metaphorically of vision as a target that beckons. Others call it *imagineering,* which is the process of creating exciting futures for a better, more just society.

Visions of shared leadership and bottom-up empowered organizations based on relationships are the new rage in organizational design. The traditional, top-down, bureaucratic, controlling model has gone the way of the typewriter. Well-oiled, predictable, clockwork systems are turning into people-centered, less precise, team-based learning organizations that are creative, unpredictable, and messy and that make up things as they go along. This transformation causes discomfort for managers who have a need to control and stay on top of all personnel and their job responsibilities. Other administrators have developed greater tolerance for risk and ambiguity; they have high boiling points and thrive on information from research, reading, and constant interaction with others about new ideas.

The new leader is a creative gadabout who helps design corporate futures through visioning and persuading others to share the vision. These new leaders in new organizations must be better prepared in the art and science of administration and futuring than those of the past. Future leaders must be exciting personalities who have a passion for what they do and can share the passion in a vision to capture the imagination and energy of others. The old saying, "You can't light a fire with a wet match," means more than ever to an aspiring leader in education and other human service organizations. "Empowerment," "transformational leadership," "quality assurance," and "shared visions" are the catchwords of the day, but unless there is an energetic, ethical, and talented visionary to light the fire of others, very few visions will be realized. Visionary leaders create ideas, goals, team loyalty, and shared values. William E. May, an authority on leadership, believes that leaders must create goals, and that means imagining the future. Well-educated charismatic leaders with ideas for improving systems to enrich the lives of others are needed today more than ever. The world is a troubled place due to the widening gap between rich and poor, the promulgation of religious beliefs that include killing nonbelievers, and the preponderance of nations lacking the resources to house, feed, and educate growing populations.

The best and most proven way to learn the skills of visionary leadership is to observe or read about those we admire. Chapter 1, "What's Leadership Got to Do With Futuring?" explains the sometimes confusing relationship between leadership and futuring. This discussion begins with an inspiring story about the link between visioning and leadership; then there are an overview of research in leadership styles, a leadership questionnaire, and information about futuring, future studies, and visioning. In addition, the reader will find an explanation of the relationships between vision and belief statements, missions, and goals. The chapter closes with a futures scenario written by a 16-year-old high school senior who clearly ties futuring to powerful leadership to make his vision happen.

Chapter 2, "Visionary Leaders I Have Known and Others I Wish I Had Known," is about seven leaders who embodied visionary leadership. Three of these leaders were my heroes from my early professional development; they shaped my life and career. The other four were visionaries who, by their acts of courage, caring, communication, and persistence, inspired millions of others to find the best in themselves and to share their visions for a better world. Each of the seven visionaries had his or her own leadership style and personality, but three key characteristics stand out to serve as guideposts for this book: They all had profound visions of service, they communicated the vision to others, and they persisted toward the vision. These three attributes must be present if a vision is to become a reality to make organizations more effective, inclusive, and supportive places. The review of the lives and contributions of these leaders offers readers a chance to gain insights into the attractive ingredients of visionary leadership and to reflect on the personal role models who have helped shape their own leadership styles and careers.

Chapter 3, "Motivating Others to Engage in Futuring," provides an overview of motivation research and its application to contemporary organizations. The futuring process is based on motivating others. When they don't understand motivation, school leaders struggle to inspire staff to meet the demands of the No Child Left Behind Act, which focuses on high-stakes exams and other rules and regulations. Because personal visions are the most motivating, the role of the visionary leader is to persuade others to rally around a shared vision of a cause beyond themselves; then they must communicate the vision to others and persist to make the vision a reality.

Chapter 4, "Making Visions Happen," includes strategies and inspirational stories about successful visionaries who transformed visions into realities and overcame the problems they faced. The importance of proper timing, good data, and financial support are presented to assist the leader in realizing the vision. The chapter ends with an account of a visionary public official with a dream for a more caring community and his leadership in making the dream happen.

Chapter 5, "Staff Development Techniques to Envision and Create Real-World Programs," contains a variety of step-by-step real-world futuring techniques to enliven workshops for learning skills to create real-world programs. Seven group and individual futuring activities are described. First is the Goodyear blimp visioning process, a very powerful activity for celebrating a national award in the year 2016. The second activity is a step-by-step application of a modified Nominal Group Technique—Cooperative Processing, along with a practical example of its application in the Huntsville, Texas, schools. Next described is an activity for envisioning schools of the future, designed to create the most child-centered and high-performing school district in America by 2015. Next there are instructions on the use of the propositional inventory and its important link to the next activity, number five—scenario writing as a planning process, ending with an interesting example. There follows a detailed explanation of the Delphi technique, and the chapter ends with an example of using a future scenario to inspire visioning.

Chapter 6, "The Visionary Leader You Can Become," provides suggestions for how leaders can create a service vision, communicate the vision, and persist to make the vision happen. Stories about Colonel David Shoup in World War II, Arlene Blum, Wilma Rudolph, and other heroes will help readers gain greater knowledge and inspiration about how to become better than they think they can be. Oliver Wendell Holmes believed that the potential within us far outweighs the accomplishments of the past or the challenges of the present and future. Thus, this final chapter challenges you, the reader, to become a leader motivated by a service vision for others, to communicate that service vision through words and actions, and never to give up on making the vision happen.

CHAPTER ONE

What's Leadership Got to Do With Futuring?

E very person reading this book aspires to become a more effective leader and is looking forward to new career challenges. While leadership and forward thinking appear to be linked, futurist Joel Barker observes that most leaders are not futurists, but they know that scanning environments and creating visions of the future will drive individual and organizational success. The most important ingredient in the leadership-futuring link is the enthusiasm of the formal leader of the organization. If leaders are excited about creating a better tomorrow for their organizations and each person in the organization, others will catch the vision and observe the leadership behaviors required to drive the vision. Remember, "You can't light a fire with a wet match." One method to inspire others about a vision and to build a fire under the staff or school board is a visual of the "generic kid" (a smiley face with big eyes and smile and a sprig of hair). This round-faced "kid" is magic in bringing focus to planning sessions, team-building activities, or staff meetings. The notion of centering on what is best for the kids or clients brings focus to the main thing—teaching and learning in education, or, in business, producing the finest product. The following story best illustrates how the leadership of a caring coach made a boy's vision come true.

MONTANA AND COACH WEIS

When we wonder about the link between the acts of leadership and visioning, we need to look no farther for the answer than the following true story. Early during the week before the Notre Dame–University of Washington football game, Cathy Mazurkiewicz contacted the Notre Dame football office to ask if a player could come to their home in Mishawaka, a suburb of South Bend, and visit with her 10-year-old son Montana, who had an inoperable brain tumor and had only hours to live . No player came, but Charlie Weis, the Notre Dame coach, did. He took time from his busy week of preparation to visit with Montana—a great young fan of Notre Dame football. Weis and Montana talked about football and about Montana's inoperable tumor. Weis shared that his daughter Hannah had some problems as well since she suffered from global development delay, a rare disorder similar to autism. Coach Weis told Montana that he was Joe Montana's roommate during his playing days at Notre Dame and about the pranks they pulled on each other. According to Tom Coyne of the Associated Press, Montana told Weis "about his love for Notre Dame football and how he wanted to make it through this game this week." Weis sat in a big chair holding Montana in his lap and helped him pass a football to his mother. Weis signed the football, "Live for today for tomorrow is always another day." Weis asked Montana if there was something he could do for him. Montana said, "Call a pass to the right on the first play in the game this Saturday." Weis promised him it would be the first play against the University of Washington on Saturday. After hugging Montana, Coach Weis left to go practice. Montana never got to see the play. He died Friday at his home.

According to Coyne's news story, Weis heard about the death and called Cathy Mazurkiewicz on Friday to assure her he would still call Montana's play. Weis said, "This game is for Montana, and the play still stands." Weis told the team about the visit. He just wanted the team to know people like Montana were out there. The real test of compassionate and ethical leadership by Weis happened when the Irish recovered a fumble inside their own one-yard line. Montana's mother wasn't sure Notre Dame would throw a pass to the right in such a vulnerable spot. Quarterback Brady Quinn asked Coach Weis what play to call. Weis said, "We have no choice—we're throwing to the right." Weis called a play where most of the Irish went left; Quinn ran right and looked for tight end Anthony Fasano on the right. Fasano caught the pass and leapt over a defender for a 13-yard gain. "It was almost like Montana was willing him to beat the defender and take it to the house," Weis said. Cathy Mazurkiewicz was happy. "It was an amazing play. Montana would have been very pleased," she said. Weis called her after the game, a 36–17 victory, and said he had a game ball signed by the team and he took it to her on Sunday. Cathy ends the story by saying, "He's a very neat man. Very compassionate. I just thanked him for using that play, no matter the consequences." This story is a clear example of how the compassionate leadership of a high-profile football coach made Montana's vision happen even though he did not get to see it. His mother told Charlie Weis that "Montana had gone to join the angels."

Thus, this first chapter will provide an overview of leadership and leadership studies and explore the links between leadership and futuring. In addition, the reader will find valuable insights into the visioning process, definitions and examples of vision, belief, and mission statements, and an explanation of how to use goal statements to motivate others to follow and realize their personal and shared visions.

THE POWER OF LEADERSHIP

Leadership remains a most intriguing concept in the course of human history. Since antiquity, leaders have created magnificent cities, powerful nations, buildings, monuments, literature, and art, e.g., Babylon, Rome, London, New York City, the Parthenon, St. Paul's Cathedral, the Guggenheim Museum in Bilbao, Michelangelo's *David*, Rembrandt's *Night Watch*, Picasso's *Two Clowns*, Virgil's *Aeneid*, and Maya Angelou's *I Know Why the Caged Bird Sings*. Inspiring stories are told about prophets, warriors, explorers, scientists, and educators whose leadership created new pathways to progress. However, from ancient times to the present, observers have remained perplexed about the actual essence of leadership and how to teach it. While researchers report multiple studies about leadership effectiveness, they find a complex mixture of myths, historical artifacts, and historical accounts that influence research findings about the characteristics of effective leaders.

Leadership scholars labor over data from investigations that have tried to determine whether leaders must be born with specific leadership traits; e.g., intelligence, judgment, aggressiveness, desire to excel, vision, energy, verbal facility, and self-confidence are important attributes for leaders. Strong evidence indicates that different leadership skills and traits are required in different situations. The behaviors and traits enabling a football coach to gain and maintain disciplined control over a team are not the same as those required of an artist mentoring young artists in mastering their disciplines. Leadership scholars Warren Bennis and Burt Nanus (1985) and Ralph Stogdill (1981) found over 350 definitions and characteristics of leadership in the literature, and they join others who challenge the lingering belief that successful leadership is a combination of innate intellectual, physical, or personality traits, that is, that only those born with these traits will become leaders. While physical size and strength are important for leadership in athletics and other activities that require strength and agility, and while innate intelligence is important to successful leadership, the puzzle remains about why some people with similar physical and intellectual traits become leaders while others do not. Leadership researchers have concluded that leaders are not born, but those who do excel as leaders display similar personal attributes and patterns of behavior.

Stephen Hawking, a leading scientist and Lucasian Professor of Mathematics at Cambridge University and victim of ALS, is confined to a wheelchair and uses a computer speech synthesizer to write and speak. His leading research proved that Einstein's general theory of relativity implied that time had a beginning in the big bang and an end in black holes. By combining relativity with quantum theory, Hawking and his colleagues created the second great scientific development in the twenty-first century. Mother Teresa and Mohandas Gandhi were not tall, imposing, aggressive leaders, but because of their spiritual and intellectual gifts they became role models for social justice and democracy around the world. These and other leaders have modeled and helped transform top-down, authoritarian rule toward bottom-up, empowered organizations stressing relationships. Hawking, Mother Teresa, and Gandhi, along with other great servant leaders, have mentored and inspired future leaders, e.g., Martin Luther King, Jr., Pope John Paul, and others. Max De Pree (1989) says it best: "Leaders are responsible for future leadership. They need to identify, develop, and nurture future leaders" (p. 14). As a result of the work of a new generation of leaders influenced by new ways of thinking about organizations (Wheatley, 1992, 2002; Kanter, 1983; Greenleaf, 1991; Glickman, 1993), organizations are gradually changing from top-down, boss-led, controlling, bureaucratic "efficiency" models with clear lines of authority and exclusive participation in decision making into organizations rich in relationships among people where trust and teamwork replace control and fear.

The literature reveals mixed evidence about why some leaders in certain situations are successful and others are dismal failures. Observers ponder why some successful leaders use a consistent style in all situations and others apply a more situational style. Research is sparse on analyzing relationships between leadership styles and institutional performance across schools, universities, and other public and private agencies. However, reports indicate that some leaders are better than others in scanning the environment and adjusting their style to address ongoing and emergent issues.

Definitions and categories of leadership styles continue to expand in the postmodern literature, which is centered on ethical leadership that opens the doors for individuals and groups that have been excluded from leadership opportunities in the past. The ethics literature takes on new meaning as society becomes more politically, racially, and economically divided. Thus, attention to moral and spiritual leadership stressing race, gender, poverty, and education grows each year. Gary Martin (2005) of Northern Arizona University indicates that much work is needed to select and prepare leaders who can help shape a just and moral society. Martin believes that a new breed of leader must step up to do the right thing for diverse communities facing injustice or exclusion from a better life. As a result, leaders in diverse settings need new skills and greater understanding of social and organizational dynamics. Thus, in these times, Martin writes, "It is difficult to find consensus on what makes an effective leader. . . . Gaining expertise in leadership requires time, commitment, an adequate knowledge base and a working plan for learning and growth" (p. 19). Martin asserts that, without a professional development plan and mentoring to help individuals learn how to solve growing social injustice and organizational personnel problems and their underlying causes, administrators will "deal with the same types of problems day after day" (p. 19). Thus, leaders must be carefully selected and given the best possible formal education, well-crafted professional development, and clinical, real-world experiences. While some individuals may inherit attributes for leadership, much more is required from environmental influences for them to wear the mantle of leadership. A mix of luck and skill is part of both successful leadership and playing a hand of cards. Some individuals are born into families with a full house of wealth and influence to begin their climb to success. Others are born into families with a pair of deuces of little wealth and influence to begin their journey. Why do some people with a pair of deuces rise to greater heights than others holding a full house? Some play the hand they are dealt and rise to become successful leaders, and others squander away their chances for success. Therefore, it is concluded that leaders are made and not born.

LEADING CHANGE

Individuals who can lead organizational change with minimal disruption rise above the rest. Leading change has never been more stressful than it is now, due to the risks of corporate and individual survival. More changes on our planet are made each second than were made in a year in 1800. According to futurist Lynn Burton (2003), "We live in an exciting, tumultuous era, during which our environment and experiences will change more than during any comparable span of history" (p. 3). These profound changes require leaders to think and act in new ways each year, day, and hour. Burton implores leaders to consider the following issues if ongoing change is to occur:

- Understanding the likelihood and possibility of different futures, and the opportunity to shape those futures.
- Enhancing flexibility in policy making and implementation.
- Broadening perspectives.
- Encouraging creative thinking (about possible, plausible, probable, and preferred futures and their potential impacts). (p. 5)

Observers agree that, even if the above suggestions are followed, the most difficult task of leaders is moving others toward personal and organizational change. We do not like change unless it benefits us personally either in financial or personal growth. The old adage that "only wet babies welcome change" holds for most people in most organizations. People can be forced to change if their jobs are on the line. Spencer Johnson (1998) in his metaphorical book *Who Moved My Cheese?* shows the pain involved in sudden change. When we are moved from one position to another or told to learn a new skill, we scream, "Who moved my cheese?" When downsizing in companies occurs, people are usually willing to learn new job responsibilities in order to take home a paycheck. Star high school quarterbacks recruited by NCAA Division I universities may be forced to move to wide receiver for playing time, and assistant professors often teach out of their special areas during their first few years on the faculty. Change is rarely welcome, but it is necessary for survival in most organizations. It seems naïve to simply recommend that teamwork and a willing spirit will solve most organizational problems. When budget crunches come and staff must be reduced or reassigned, tough decisions must be made for company or school-district solvency.

Thus, the most difficult skill is leading organizational change when people are fearful of losing their jobs, being demoted, and losing their sense of value as individuals. Kurt Lewin (1948) provided a profound process to help understand how to bring about change. He said leaders must break the equilibrium in individual "force fields" by an "unfreezing" process. That is, leaders with foresight and influence must help others let go of old attitudes, values, and behaviors tightly held. Once the mental thaw begins, it is possible to introduce change and begin stressing new values, attitudes, and behaviors. Once the thaw has occurred and new values, attitudes, and behaviors begin, it is time for "refreezing." This helps to protect and ensure key attitudes toward long-range retention of the changes. Otherwise, one tends to slip back into old ways of doing and thinking (Cunningham, 1982).

In spite of the pain associated with leading change, most observers conclude that working in collaboration to build trusting relationships, creating clear and inclusive communication networks, empowering others, and developing leaders within the organization can reduce the amount of pain in change. Unless people are included in the vision and guided through the reasons and steps for change, the resistance will increase. Creating systems to manage change is a gradual process; managers can lead incremental change over time and lead others through the change process. Leaders must never lose sight of the power of human relationships; they may need to work with one person at a time in guiding organizational change. An effective strategy in leading change is best summed up by Ken Blanchard in his *Whale Done* (2002). After observing Sea World trainers change the behavior of killer whales at Sea World, Blanchard concludes that the power of positive relationships is the key. He writes, "Everybody knows that accentuating the positive works best. But what do you do when somebody does something that has a negative impact? That's where Chuck and the Sea World trainers opened my eyes. Instead of focusing energy, as most of us do, on what went wrong, they redirect that energy toward a positive outcome" (p. ix). It is not wise to slap a 4,000-pound killer whale for making a mistake—it may be our last leadership act! Only through patience and positive reinforcement can we lead whales or people to successful performance. When individuals find that they are engaged in the jobs or roles they best fit and are offered positive support and state-of-the art professional training, they welcome change much more easily than others forced into unfamiliar roles they are not encouraged or prepared to play. While this advice may not apply to all change pressures, it can bring about positive attitudes about change better than other, more Machiavellian power methods. Change is painful and can bring on mourning for the good old days, but not to change is to stagnate and take others with you.

Research on creating change in most urban school districts reveals that successful change is not the result of simply providing more financial resources for instruction and computers for every student. Rather, it is the result of focusing on one educator, student, or parent at a time. A recent study of urban school dropouts revealed that unless the CEO established a systems approach to reducing the number of dropouts, little progress was made. None of the ten urban districts in the study was meeting all the needs that a successful dropout program would have. The district leadership seemed to be aware that the dropout problem was the skunk under the porch: Everyone knew it was there, but it was rarely seen and only mentioned in passing. The researchers concluded that in urban districts where minimizing dropouts is a high priority, CEOs are displaying systems leadership and appointing key administrators to collaborate with community, state, and federal agencies and individuals to create strategies to improve the dropout problem one student at a time (Hoyle & Collier, 2005).

John Simmons (2005) sums up what policy makers know, but fail to implement in transforming urban and other poorly performing schools. He believes that districts that have clear goals, open communication with parents and teaching staff, specific objectives, and cost-effective policies and practices aligned to accelerate student learning will change with the times. These changes can be facilitated by concentrating on four strategies:

1. Create leaders at every level. Leadership is shared among teachers, parents, and administrators.

2. Transform the structure and culture of the district. Move to the collaborative model supporting solutions proposed by those closest to the problem.

3. Improve instruction. Administrators must support high-quality professional development to help teachers apply more effective instructional strategies and help one another to meet the diverse needs of all students.

4. Engage parents and make funding adequate and equitable. Strong partnerships with parents and equitable funding are essential for accelerating and sustaining the transformation process. (Simmons, p. 18)

Change occurs when individuals have common beliefs; are given advanced, correct information; are provided strong professional development to adjust to organizational change; and are encouraged to work together for a common cause. Change theory based on changing the system to emphasize the talents and goals of people first and the goals of the organization second holds strong potential to guide leaders in transforming schools, public agencies, and universities to adapt to our changing world.

LEADERSHIP STRATEGIES AND STYLES

Observers of leadership practices find that categorizing leadership styles is difficult. Gary Crow, Joseph Matthews, and Lloyd McCleary (1996) summarize major leadership themes in the literature:

1. Leadership as a personal quality.

2. Leadership as a type of behavior.

3. Leadership depending on the situation.

4. Leadership as relational.

5. Leadership as a moral quality for systemic improvement.

However, the most common leadership labels in the literature and the choice for this book include the following four categories: authoritarian, transactional, participative, and transformational (Hoy & Miskel, 2005).

Authoritarian Leaders

Authoritarian leaders use Machiavellian principles to manipulate people and use political power unfettered by traditional ethical norms. Niccolo Machiavelli (1469–1527) published the famous book *The Prince* (1532/1992), which became the guide to acquiring and maintaining political power and learning strategies to become a despot to rule over others. Former Italian dictator Benito Mussolini used ideas from *The Prince* to become *Il Duce* (leader) and led a coup d'etat in Rome to concentrate power into the hands of the Fascist Party. However, Mussolini's thirst for power and his military defeats left Italy in ruins, turning thousands of hungry homeless people against his ruthless authoritarian leadership. He was captured wearing a dress and hiding with his mistress in the back of a small Italian truck attempting to flee to Switzerland. Mussolini was tried in court and executed in Milan, Italy, on April 28, 1945.

While most authoritarian leaders are not power-hungry despots who destroy a nation, they display a need to control the organization by expecting unquestioned obedience to management rather than encouraging individual free expression and shared decision making. This style hearkens back to the scientific management of Fredrick Taylor (1947) and other efficiency figures that emphasize production over people and to McGregor's (1985) Theory X style of leading, which assumes people are lazy and must be forced to work. That is, people must be closely supervised and rewarded or punished according to their level of productivity. Authoritarian leaders worship traditional top-down, divide-and-conquer line-and-staff organizational charts with clear levels of authority and communication patterns. Two cartoons best illustrate and remind us of the predominance of authoritarian leaders in all types of organizations: Mr. Dithers continues to drop-kick Dagwood, and Pointy Hair continues his acrimony with Dilbert and the other office workers.

Take-Charge School Leaders. When school boards faced with low test scores hire "take-charge" superintendents to "right the ship," authoritarian leadership and forced followership rule the entire school district. Findings are mixed about what leadership styles are superior in terms of increasing test scores across school situations, but research into best practices finds that some leaders are better than others in scanning the environment and adjusting their leadership styles to address problems of student achievement and meeting the mandates of the No Child Left Behind Act (NCLB). Since this act became law, there is growing evidence that the pressure for higher student and teacher performance increases each school year, and authoritarian leadership styles dominate and control the curriculum, instruction, and testing. While this leadership style may result in improved efficiency and test scores, teachers and school administrators warn that narrowing the curriculum to teach to the test restricts teacher creativity and can have a negative effect on preparing students to face new problems and learn creative thinking skills to adjust to the dramatic changes in a digital and competitive world.

Law Enforcers or Peace Officers? When city councils decide to "get tough on crime," they instruct the current police chiefs to increase police visibility, establish a tighter teen curfew, and increase the number of citations for a variety of reasons. If these more stringent steps are not taken to the satisfaction of the city council, the discussion turns to finding a new chief who will enforce their tougher policies to cut the crime rate by using a more authoritarian leadership style. There is general agreement among scholars that authoritarian leadership is necessary in emergency situations or when organizational goals are not being met, but over the long haul authoritarian leaders create more problems than individuals in the organization can solve.

Since 9/11 the American people have a new appreciation for the heroism of our law enforcement officers and firefighters. They put themselves in harm's way for people they do not know each day and hour. In some cases, these servants for safety must take aggressive action to avert dangerous situations, but otherwise they work to make communities better places for children, schools, and families. In working with the California Commission on Peace

Officer Standards and Training (POST), I have been impressed with the high quality of the law enforcement leaders with the highway patrol and the city and county police forces and with their many programs for children and youth. These varied programs in collaboration with schools, churches, and youth centers are designed to help young people become good citizens and gain a greater understanding of the role of law enforcement in creating safe communities.

Transactional Leaders

Transactional leaders require the integration of organizational goals and expectations with the needs of the people doing the work. This model is based on the dual organization, where the bureaucratic side has natural conflicts with the professional one. This people-versus-organization balance is very clear in the Getzels-Guba social systems model (1957), which is a two-dimensional transactional model. The model delineates the differences between the *idiographic*—representing the needs and dispositions of individuals, and the *nomothetic*—representing the goals of the organization, and it describes the transactions and potential conflicts between the two. This model displays the dynamics between the needs of people and the purposes of the organization. The workers may feel that the production goals of management are beyond their abilities, training, equipment, and energy. This conflict or stress found in organizations of all kinds is important for management to understand to maintain a critical balance between staff morale and production levels. Theorists agree that a proper balance of dynamic tension between organizational goals for production and the personalities and needs of employees can be healthy. This conflict is compared to the grit in a mollusk shell that produces a beautiful pearl. Excess grit can cause abnormal pearls, just as too much control and pressure in organizations can cause poor production.

James Macgregor Burns (1978) observes that transactional leaders motivate workers by offering rewards for organizational productivity. Robert Owens (2000) writes that "transactional educational leaders can and do offer jobs, security, tenure, favorable ratings, and more in exchange for the support, cooperation, and compliance of followers" (p. 209). Transactional leadership reflects the reality of most work places and appears to dominate most organizations, including schools and universities.

High-Stakes Exams. Public school superintendents and principals facing the pressures of accountability for higher student performance on high-stakes tests and NCLB criteria find themselves balancing the spinning plates of interpersonal relationships with teachers along with the plates of higher performance demanded by the community. One Florida superintendent told this writer that he wants the teachers and administrators on each campus to know that he cares about them and their families, but on the other hand if the student test scores do not improve the school board will have his head on one of those spinning plates. His vision statement is "Whatever It Takes." My work with the leadership team emphasized the need to set higher standards for teachers and students but never to neglect the interpersonal communication, kindness, and dignity necessary for the teachers to share the vision of "Whatever It Takes." If this balance is maintained between the administrators and teachers, the tension between the goals of the organization and the needs of the staff can be viewed as a positive dimension that drives a school or corporation to higher performance.

Each semester at Texas A&M University, this writer teaches a graduate seminar on leadership and organizational behavior, and the students face the dreaded midterm exam. As the exam time approaches, several of the advanced doctoral students will ask that the exam be a take-home, or they ask to be allowed to substitute a research paper covering the test items. Each semester my response is same: The test is nonnegotiable because the course content encompasses the cradle of the disciplines of educational administration and leadership. And if they fail to master this material, they may not pass the required comprehensive written and oral exams. Each semester the grades range from 80 percent to 90+ percent, and the students find the material very valuable at comprehensive exam time. Thus, graduate school and other organizations apply transactional leadership where compliance with important procedures for successful performance is a good trade-off for the employee and the organization.

Participative Leaders

Participative leaders view organizations as humans working together to accomplish tasks rather than building artificial barriers that force productivity. Participative leaders espouse participative leadership and view schools and other organizations as social systems in which people's social needs are valued equally with the organization's goals for high performance. Rosa Beth Kanter, Tom Sergiovanni, Terry Deal, and many others stress participative leadership in building productive organizations that balance the need for productivity with the personalities and needs of people. These scholars observe that, if management projects authoritarian or certain transactional styles of leadership, the system is perceived by employees to be impersonal, ruled by fear hidden in the chain of command, and that they are mere pawns for management. Employees are told when to work, how to work, and how to account for their work. Unless participative leadership prevails, management blames individuals for mistakes rather than improving the system they run.

In contrast, participative leaders communicate, provide professional development, delegate, encourage diversity, and encourage collective effort to seek quality in each task and final product. This collaborative process brings a family atmosphere to the workplace and creates respect for the contributions of each member. Mike Cargill, superintendent of the Bryan, Texas, Independent School District, exemplifies participative leadership by encouraging input from central office staff, district administrators, teachers, parents, and college and university faculty, students, and staff. Cargill's humble welcoming spirit of participation is producing higher student achievement, lower numbers of dropouts, higher teacher morale, and a smooth working relationship with the board of education. While planning new schools, including a new high school, and with growing numbers of low-income students entering the district each year, Cargill and the school board are moving together as a team of eight to meet the challenges of future enrollments and higher costs with less funding. In addition, Hurricanes Katrina and Rita led many evacuees to the Bryan school house doors. The first persons to welcome these displaced and frightened students were Mike Cargill and members of his team. Mike Cargill and participative leadership are synonymous.

Transformational Leaders

Transformational leaders create an environment where persons are empowered to fulfill their highest professional needs and are encouraged to become members of a supportive learning community.

Transformational leaders are servants to others and guide them in creating and embracing a vision for the organization that inspires and brings forth top performance, diversity of thought, and inclusion of all races and ideologies. Subsumed in this style are moral leadership (Fullen, 2003; Sergiovanni, 1992), leading with love (Hoyle, 2002a), leadership for social justice (Tillman et al., 2003), and spiritual leadership (Wheatley, 2002).

Moral Leadership. Moral leadership is based on dignity and respect for the rights of others to self-determination within moral boundaries of the organization. Schools with moral leadership focus on the welfare of each student, teacher, and staff member who shares in the belief that the school family should work to inspire higher levels of trust and commitment to every child and each other in the school community. Thomas Sergiovanni (1992) says it best: "When moral authority drives leadership practice, the principal is at the same time a leader of leaders, follower of ideas, minister of values, and servant to the followership" (p. 38). Leaders guided by these moral principals can expect greater organizational productivity because employees are motivated to take personal responsibility in assuring the quality of the entire organization. The works of Edwards Deming (1982, 1993) paved the way in caring about the employees and using good data to improve the organizational system by basing it on moral principles of trusting employees rather than blaming them for failures. This leadership style encourages all employees to share the organizational vision or aim and embrace the larger context of the organization in society, and it provides encouragement and professional development for all team members. Max De Pree (1989) expressed the need for transformational leadership thus: "Without understanding the cares, yearnings and struggles of the human spirit, how can anyone presume to lead a group of people across the street?" (p. 221).

Unconditional Love and Leadership. Leading with unconditional love is linked to transformational leadership. This leadership style reaches beyond leading with heart, soul, and morality and moves on the concept of love in an attempt to reteach the lessons of history's great leaders. The most powerful leaders in history are remembered not for their positions, wealth, or number of publications, but for their unconditional love for others. Leading with love revisits the ideas that guide human kindness, social justice, and servant leadership and rediscovers ways to replace anger, violence, mistrust, and hatred with love. The Greeks used the word *agape* as the highest form of love. *Agape* is unselfish love, love of unlovable people, and love that overwhelms animosity in schools, universities, and other organizations (Hoyle, 2002a).

Social Justice and Leadership. Closely linked to leading with love is leadership for social justice. According to Tillman et al. (2003), leadership in social justice "enables us to have a way to create momentum to bring people together who have worked for equity. . . . Social justice means more than equity; it means an activist, interventionist stance" (p. 85). This postmodernist position has heightened the need for research in educational administration and other social sciences to examine its theories to ensure that new voices are included in the literature and that these voices influence school and university administrator and faculty search committees in their efforts toward greater inclusiveness, equity, and justice.

Spiritual Leadership. Some scholars believe that the capstone of transformational leadership is spirituality. Deepak Chopra (2002) observes that leaders are the symbolic souls of the organizations they lead, and great leaders respond from the higher levels of spirit and grow from inside out. The spiritual and administrative sides are of equal importance when guiding a school or university dedicated to helping each student become a successful, ethical individual. Spiritual leaders assert that without a spiritual side, a leader lacks depth in understanding human needs and can destroy morale with a thoughtless comment or action. Missing the spiritual dimension of leadership can lead to children's failure in school by ignoring the child's background or family circumstance. To ignore children's failure and injustice is spiritless leadership (Hoyle, 2002b). Spiritual leadership is encouraging others to seek the highest vision, reaching for the highest human endeavors, and serving before being served. Writers concur that this is the most sought-after form of transformational leadership.

The evolution from top-down authoritarian to transformational leadership is occurring in America's corporations, agencies, schools, and universities. To facilitate this change, refined research methods are needed to seek connections among leadership styles, staff morale, and human performance. Until research provides clearer evidence that newer forms of leadership actually promote greater equity, empowerment, morality, love, and higher performance, corporations, agencies, schools, and universities will continue to rely more on authoritarian and transactional leadership. Perhaps in time when research and best practice provide support for transformational leadership it can move to center stage .

The following self-report instrument may assist you in gaining insight into your leadership style.

Directions: Circle the number that best measures your self-perception on each leadership characteristic. Add all the circled numbers to find your score.

As a leader I am . . .	Always		Usually		Sometimes		Rarely
1. Caring	6	5	4	3	2	1	0
2. Optimistic	6	5	4	3	2	1	0
3. Creative	6	5	4	3	2	1	0
4. Forgiving	6	5	4	3	2	1	0
5. Patient	6	5	4	3	2	1	0
6. Visionary	6	5	4	3	2	1	0
7. Respectful	6	5	4	3	2	1	0
8. Honest	6	5	4	3	2	1	0
9. Selfless	6	5	4	3	2	1	0
10. Loyal	6	5	4	3	2	1	0
11. A listener	6	5	4	3	2	1	0
12. Persistent	6	5	4	3	2	1	0
13. Energetic	6	5	4	3	2	1	0
14. Collaborative	6	5	4	3	2	1	0
15. Diplomatic	6	5	4	3	2	1	0
16. Enthusiastic	6	5	4	3	2	1	0
17. Dependable	6	5	4	3	2	1	0
18. Persuasive	6	5	4	3	2	1	0
19. Articulate	6	5	4	3	2	1	0
20. Ethical	6	5	4	3	2	1	0

Score: 120–110 = Transformational/Participative Leader
109–71 = Transactional Leader
70 or below = Authoritative Leader

What Is Futuring Anyway?

Futuring is an intellectual process of peering into the future through creative visioning, speculation, brainstorming, and disciplined research. The art and science of the study of *futurism, futuristics,* or *future studies* (the three terms are used interchangeably) has emerged as a respected field of inquiry in universities, corporations, government, military, law enforcement, agriculture, and other organizations and fields. The search for a more understandable and successful tomorrow is the quest of most humans, and the need to anticipate and manage a brighter future is a universal need. Obviously, not all look to a brighter future in this life. Since 9/11 and the U.S. response in Iraq, numerous religious fanatics who believe that their reward in is another life choose to strap bombs to their bodies and end their earthly future and the future of innocent people. Thus, futuring depends on anticipating and managing change but also counts on continuity and respect for others and their future.

Future studies has grown from a topic for isolated groups of social scientists, novelists, and artists to achieve widespread interest, and now there are organized groups that study it, such as the World Future Society with over 40,000 members. This global interest has moved futurism away from its popular image, which includes reading tea leaves, fortune-telling, palm reading, and crystal balls, to sophisticated Web systems for trend analyses, multiple scenario creations, and futures gaming on almost every topic. The "vision thing" is thrown about with reckless abandon and can lose its power as a result. Some people, such as Steve Jobs, I. M. Pei, Bill Gates, Oprah Winfrey, Hillary Clinton, and Jimmy Carter, have vision. Others may never have it no matter how hard they try. People tend to limit themselves and fail to achieve their dreams because they limit their vision and do not believe in themselves enough. In the same vein, an old coach told his hurdler, "Never build hurdles in your mind, because hurdles on the track are much smaller than the hurdles in your mind." Moreover, the adage "if you believe you can or you can't, you are right either way" is the truth.

Although futurists never attempt to predict the future, they can design alternative futures based on different data sets; then they use creative thinking processes to solve social and technical problems at the local or global levels. According to Ed Cornish, founder of the World Future Society, and others, futurists focus on three key areas as a foundation for forecasting possible, probable, or unlikely futures. *One,* they believe that the world and all of its systems and inhabitants are interconnected and thus dependent on each other for survival. *Two,* futurists are focused on time as a critical factor in choice. They believe that to change the course of events, one begins now, not next week or next month. The future of the environment, the quality of the air, water, and food supply, and human interactions is not determined in five years but now, today! *Three,* ideas of the future are a driving motivational force for improving the lot of humankind. For example, imagine in 2025 an ideal, safe, self-sustaining community for 50,000 people with adequate food supplies, health care, education, and quality jobs. Imagine a world where children around the world no longer sleep on the ground and cry themselves to sleep due to hunger, and envision each child in a warm clean house with adequate food with available heath care.

Based on these three areas, futurists strive to anticipate what may occur. Some events are easier to forecast than others. For instance, demographics are relatively easy to predict because data are accessible on world, national, and local population trends, and we know about those already born. The U.S. population is over 285 million, its birth rate is 14.2 per 1000 population, and its average life expectancy is 77.12 years. America is 52 percent Protestant, 25 percent Catholic, 1.3 percent Jewish, and 0.5 percent Muslim. The U.S. population includes 72 percent whites, and this figure will decrease to 64 percent by 2020. By 2060, the country will be evenly divided between white and nonwhite populations.

World population is 6.8 billion, and population projections for 2025 range from 8.2 billion to 11.4 billion, depending on numerous factors including adequate health care, the AIDS epidemic in Africa, and global water and food distribution. By 2025, the population of Africa will be three times that of Europe (1.58 billion versus 500+ million). Behind these alarming statistics lies the reality: Each human being requires daily 2,000 to 3,000 calories of food and 4 ½ pints of water. Obviously this need is not being met for many in Africa and other troubled spots in the world today (Kennedy, 1993; Population Reference Bureau, 2006).

Other trends in economics, technology, agriculture, medicine, education, social psychology, and religious belief systems remain very difficult to forecast, much less manage. Because 80 percent of the new technologies necessary to compete in world markets have not been discovered yet, because China is now a member of the World Trade Organization (Friedman, 2005), and because other nations are competing with the United States and Europe in offshoring and outsourcing, multiple scenarios and new research methods are necessary to design visions of the future and act on them. The futurist community continues a quest for more sophisticated research methods and techniques, and some see the possibility of a genuine science of the future—not a natural science like chemistry or biology, but a social science like sociology and anthropology. According to Cornish (2004), futurists count on some continuity in human activity and organizations as a launching pad for what can happen in the future. He writes, "If everything constantly changed, we could not possibly know anything about the future or anything else, for that matter. Though change is normally our focus, we have to recognize that much remains constant, and it is this continuity that allows us to anticipate future events and plan what we should do" (p. 48). Therefore, to get a better feel for the future in a complex, competitive world, we must make some assumptions about how future studies or futurism can guide our visioning.

Assumptions of Futuring

Assumption #1. To affect the future, we must begin now! It is impossible to change course on a roller coaster because about all we can do is hang on until it comes to a stop. We must assume that we can change our course as a captain would steer a boat to the harbor or down a rapidly moving river. The swifter the stream and the larger the boat, the sooner the steering must begin for the ship to arrive safely at its moorings. We must begin now to avoid running aground.

Assumption #2. We must remain flexible about the number of assumptions we consider because false assumptions can lead us in the wrong direction and harm people, property, or morale. It is wise to analyze multiple data sets and consider a range from the most pessimistic to the optimistic alternatives to avoid pitfalls along the way (Bishop, 1994). There is an assumption that the United States needs to drill for oil in the wilds of Alaska to reduce our dependence on foreign oil, but the assumption may prove to be wrong because of possible irreparable damage to the environment. The assumption that distance education is equal in quality to traditional education may prove to be correct, but current research does not necessarily support that assumption. Alternative assumptions are very important in attempting to alter organizations, environments, and people.

Assumption #3. An alternative future that is owned only by its creator is doomed to failure unless it is viewed and clearly described by those who must make the vision happen. When dedicated educators believes that "all kids can learn," they must work to make that vision happen by changing beliefs among teachers and the community that children of poverty cannot overcome years of poverty and abuse. This assumption, based on research and best practice, begins with an inspiring vision followed by strategies to improve the system to overcome the status quo and change prevailing belief systems. One person's vision driven by research and love can move mountains and prove that poor children of color and those with language differences can learn at the highest levels. To assume that crime is a form of human variation and inevitable is to turn away from the power of building lives one at a time through collaborative community action.

Assumptions about what we know and the continuing search for knowledge inspire Allen Tough (2003) to see futuring as "rapidly expanding your efforts to develop future-oriented knowledge, ideas, insights, understanding, visions, and wisdom. You need to know far more about world problems, social change, potential futures, and . . . caring about future generations" (p. 129). Futurists cannot predict the future in detail, but the field of study enables us to anticipate problems along the way and provides trend analyses and techniques and skills to guide organizations in achieving long-term goals. William Shakespeare knew the power of futuring when he penned,

There is a tide in the affairs of men

Which taken at the flood, leads on to fortune;

Omitted, all the voyage of their life

Is bound in shallows and in miseries.

On such a full sea are we now afloat,

And we must take the current when it serves,

Or lose our ventures.

—William Shakespeare,
Julius Caesar, Act IV, Scene 3

Studying the Future

Futurism requires individuals to peer into the unknown, analyze trend data, and take the risks required to step into the unknown with scenarios of what may occur and what to avoid. Since 1960, more and more universities have been offering courses on future studies, while government, business, and the military are engaged in futuring processes to anticipate the purchasing habits of customers, the educational needs of citizens of all ages, and the housing needs of growing populations. They are looking for ways to manage food supply and distribution to millions, health systems to serve greater numbers, and technological advances in communications, trade, and travel.

The World Futures Society reminds us that futurism has grown into a coherent body of techniques and knowledge known as *futurism, futuring,* or *future studies.* Thinking about what is beyond the next curve is more important than ever before due to the abilities of the Internet, wireless communications, and biotechnologies to increase the rate at which change occurs, possibly causing environmental damage or facilitating terrorism on a scale unimaginable before 9/11. Thus, futuring is the act of seeing and feeling and anticipating alternative futures that are either in the near (5–10 years away), middle (11–20 years away), or far future (21–50 years away). Futuring can be done by individuals or groups depending on the need. The futuring process begins with an idea or beliefs that can range from the probable or realistic to the improbable or unrealistic. Explorers of the future are time travelers that, according to Cornish (2004), need to learn the following seven lessons:

1. Prepare for what you will face in the future.

2. Anticipate future needs.

3. Use poor information when necessary.

4. Expect the unexpected.

5. Think long term as well as short term.

6. Dream productively.

7. Learn from your predecessors. (pp. 1–7)

FUTURING AND VISIONING

The terms *futuring* and *visioning* are frequently used interchangeably in the literature and in this book. While futuring reaches beyond visioning in terms of strategic planning to set the futuring process in motion, either term inspires individuals and groups to create desired futures or avoid them. The late futurist H. G. Wells showed he knew the importance of attaining new knowledge about global problems, human behavior, and new technologies when he stated, "Human history becomes more and more a race between education and catastrophe." That is, a positive future is the result of learning about global change, geopolitical processes, and collaboration to solve growing environmental degradation and human conflict. Visioning and futuring stimulate the intellectual and creative corners of the mind. Bill Gates chased his vision from his garage workshop to the megacorporation called Microsoft. His vision enticed other entrepreneurs and venture capitalists to cast their future with Gates, and many of them became millionaires. Margaret Fuller, a transcendentalist writer in the 1840s, wrote about equal rights for women in American life. Her works challenged male domination over women in higher education and society. Rosa Parks envisioned a free and just society by refusing an order to give her bus seat to a white person. Her defiant refusal to be denied equal treatment changed the nation. President John F. Kennedy had a vision that changed our world forever in 1960 by declaring that the United States would have a man on the moon by the end of the decade. His vision inspired the nation to allocate the funding, select and train astronauts, and place Neil Armstrong on the moon in 1969. Peter Senge (1990) reminds us that for a vision to be effective for organizations it must be shared by others and they must feel committed to making the vision happen. When a vision is realized, it is the result of total commitment by individuals who carry the responsibilities required for completion and success.

Vision Statements

A vision statement, to be significant, must inspire others to strive for their highest spiritual and professional ideal, and it must capture the imagination and energy of others in the school district, agency, or business. The school executive leads the way by sharing his or her vision for the district and openly encouraging others to improve the wording for more inclusive acceptance of the key ideas in the vision statement. The statement should inspire the hearts and minds of the entire district staff—those that do the teaching, counseling, mentoring, nursing, food serving, bus transportation, custodial and maintenance services, and administration. Clement Bezold, president of the Institute for Alternative Futures, says that a vision must address the heart; that is, "A vision is a compelling statement of the preferred future that an organization or community wants to create. Visions move and inspire us by stating why we are working together, what higher contribution flows from our efforts, and what we are striving to become. Vision development is the most powerful way to clarify where you would like change to go" (as quoted in Cornish, 2004, p. 75). In other words, "Visionary leadership is knowing how to inspire hearts, ignite minds, and move hands to create tomorrow" (Hoyle, 2002a, p. 29). A vision statement must be brief, inclusive, and inspiring. Hallmark cards say it well: "When you care enough to send the very best." This is one school district's vision statement: "The [district] acts to guide and inspire all students to reach their highest achievement and moral development." This is the reason schools and educators exist. Everything else is peripheral.

Belief Statements

In recent years, futurist and visionary leaders have been including *Belief Statements* in their planning with others to strengthen the links between vision and mission statements. Belief statements represent the core values held by individuals affected by the school district or other organizations. One educator told this writer that belief statements that help all kids succeed in life must mean enough to those who write them that "they would be willing to fight to see them fulfilled." Individuals in different communities or organizations may hold certain core values that vary from those of others. However, Robert Kidder writes that most people around the world embrace *honesty, fairness, compassion, respect,* and *responsibility* (as cited in Hoyle, 2002b). Thus, in spite of religious, cultural, and ethnic diversity, belief statements can be developed to create a common ground in academic, social, and ethical excellence for all students and their development. (In Chapter 5 of this text the reader will find a thorough step-by-step visioning and belief statement process that was applied in the Huntsville, Texas, Independent School District to create belief statements that will guide policy decisions for the coming years. A Council of Excellence whose 90 members were selected from the community was involved in the year-long visioning process and created the beliefs.)

Mission Statements

A mission statement is developed by the group to explain to external individuals or clients what the organization does and how it carries out its tasks. The mission statement is more detailed than the vision and belief statements because it should include multiple missions and processes for the customers or clients. Guided by the vision and belief statements, what does the organization do to develop a comprehensive inclusive mission? What mission statement is in place to ensure that this vision and belief statements are to be realized? As an example, the mission statement of a school district might include the following:

> The mission of [district] is to provide multiple learning and personal development opportunities for all students by employing outstanding educators and staff who possess the skills and leadership qualities to provide the highest quality academic and other activities to promote student development now and for future careers.
>
> To ensure mission success, the school board, superintendent, and all employees are dedicated to providing the required curriculum and other learning opportunities that will prepare graduates to succeed in higher education, the work force, the military, and other future endeavors. The [district] will provide a complete range of learning opportunities for all students, and will ensure that benchmark curriculum materials, teaching methods, and student assistance are in place and that every student's progress is monitored and the student's parents or guardians are kept informed about the student's academic progress and personal development.

The mission statement can go into greater detail about the required state curriculum at each grade level and can provide information about curriculum guides, vertical alignment of teaching, and assessing the curriculum and instruction grade by grade. It can include additional teaching strategies and student intervention strategies that will be provided to offer every student the opportunity for academic and personal success in school. The mission statement must be comprehensive enough to include the why, what, and when of all school instructional and cocurricular programs and processes, including those for assessment and for student safety and well-being, in a readable and jargon-free format.

Goal Statements

Goal statements are the detailed, specific statements directed at making the vision (aim) happen—they are linked to belief statements, and they are designed to carry out the mission. Goal statements include specific measurable objectives or enablers that determine if the benchmarks are being reached and that find the discrepancies if they are not. In public education, all states have developed forms of high-stakes tests that are designed to assess whether students may advance to the next grade or, in most states, whether they may receive a high school diploma. Thus, with heightened pressure to drill students on the high-stakes test objectives and meet the required standards of the No Child Left Behind Act, curriculum objectives take on a whole new and stressful meaning. However, evidence is growing that, while teaching to the test may limit the broader creative and problem-solving abilities of students, test-driven instruction has improved the academic performance of children of color, children who live in poverty, and children for whom English is a second language. Thus, there is some skepticism about creating narrow, goal-driven instructional systems based on too many goals and objectives that may or may not measure the most important elements in helping students become confident problem solvers and creative thinkers (Popham, 2003).

In any field of endeavor, there is little reason to initiate a plan if teachers and students are overwhelmed by the number of goals and objectives that may not be measurable. If a public school improvement plan has instructional goals that cannot be accurately assessed in a given time period, or if the plan fails to provide teachers with test data on a regular basis to assist students in reaching their maximum academic and personal potential, then steps must be taken to adjust the number and clarity of the goals and the formative assessment processes to make the system appropriate for all students. Well-developed goal statements are instrumental in creating a successful outcome-measured system. If the goal statements closely align with the vision and mission statements and are the basis for both formative and summative assessment, there is strong evidence that a school district, a public agency, or a university will serve clients well. Goals quickly lose their value if they can be reached with little effort or if the goals are unclear or unreachable.

Figure 1.1 sums up the elements described in this section and their proper sequence in making a vision happen.

CONCLUSIONS

Great leaders possess a deep grasp of human behavior and the forces impacting change. Moreover, these great leaders embrace a democratic sense of why people need to be informed and given equal access to educational, social, and economic systems to earn dignity, provide for their families, and contribute to the general welfare of the nation. While some individuals appear to be destined for leadership due to family status or wealth, most leaders are incubated by families, teachers, counselors, school administrators, religious leaders, coaches, scout leaders, university faculty and staff, and mentors of all ages and backgrounds. It is among these individuals that

Figure 1.1   The Four Essential Elements for Making Visions Happen

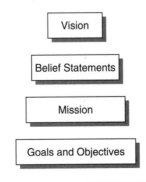

leaders observe effective and noneffective leadership styles and learn the value of compassion for those they lead.

The standard authoritarian leadership style is definitely moving over for leaders displaying more participatory, transactional, and transformational styles. While these person-centered styles are emerging in the literature and among executives striving to lead organizations to success and solvency, research is underway to refine the attitude and methods that lead to success. Leadership gurus Warren Bennis, Rensis Likert, Henry Mintzberg, Rosabeth Kanter, and Peter Drucker all have pronounced the death of the dictator in leadership studies. People do not want or need bosses who demand that they become higher performers with a strong commitment to the organization. People need and deserve leaders who care about them as individuals, who recognize that they have lives outside the organization, and who know that the people they're leading want to find a strong sense of accomplishment, be recognized for good work, and become more productive professionals each month and year. Leaders with a passion for their organizations and a belief in the dignity of each employee have already moved in the right direction toward success. If these leaders are also visionaries who use futuring strategies to inspire others to accomplish specific and more difficult goals, and who help align the forces in the system toward the aims of the organization, great things happen.

Leading Fortune 500 companies, top universities, schools, city governments, law enforcement units, public and private agencies, and sports teams striving to become the best must create and share inspiring visions of greatness and compelling belief statements to guide others toward accomplishing their missions. The heart and soul of leadership is inspiring people to reach greater heights in their individual performance and encouraging a collective passion for producing the highest-quality products. Thus, effective leadership inspires others through a vision for greater performance and guides the organization beyond what others believe possible. According to Cunningham and Cordeiro (2005), "Leadership concentrates on vision, the direction an organization should take. It draws others into the active pursuit of strategic goals" (p. 155). Finally, Grant Teaff (1994) sums leadership up best: "Leadership is physically and mentally tiring. And most often, worthwhile goals are the hardest to attain and take the longest. Therefore, mental and physical endurance is essential to a successful leader" (p. 206).

A Scenario: Leadership with Vision

This chapter concludes with a scenario written by a 16-year-old high school student who understood the important link between vision and leadership:

My name is Armando and it is now 2020, and I am sitting on the fourth deck of Kyle Field football stadium at Texas A&M University watching a football game between the Aggies and the Texas Longhorns. I am proud of this fourth deck since I built it two years ago to help accommodate over 100,000 fans who wish to follow their national powerhouse team. I not only built this deck, but I also built a geodesic dome over the entire central campus to preserve the buildings from the acid rain from the air pollution caused by extended use of fossil fuels and to maintain a climate-controlled educational environment. I also created alternative fuels from grain and hydrogen that would help reverse pollution, but the petroleum industry and lobby remained too powerful to consider my cheaper and clearer fuels.

Oh! Hold it while I use the instant replay binoculars I designed in 2007. Yes, that blind referee missed another call in favor of the enemy! After leaving high school, I entered Texas A&M University and earned degrees in architecture and engineering and went to work with a large engineering firm. After two boring years playing the corporate loyalty and nonrisk game, I stole their best ideas and formed my own company. I guess you would call me an entrepreneur. I hired several imaginative risk-takers who were educated about future studies, and the results have been remarkable! My group can create a new town in two or three weeks in practically any spot on earth; we are growing food on the ocean floor and in outer space; we can literally feed the hungry of the world, provide health care to third-world nations, and provide resources for improved educational opportunities for all urban and rural poor children and youth. Along the way, in 2012, I received a law degree from Harvard University to help me deal with the litigious society of the time. I am pleased with my life and the capability to help others less fortunate. When I think back to my time in high school, I had little hope for an education since my grandmother was my only support. People helped, and now I can return that love and kindness. I plan to move into the housing industry soon and take the ideas from former President Jimmy Carter and help build thousands of Habitat for Humanity homes. Much remains to be done, but with hard work, vision, and a lot of leadership, I shall prevail.

CHAPTER TWO

Visionary Leaders I Have Known and Others I Wish I Had Known

Visionary leadership is knowing how to inspire hearts, ignite minds, and move hands to create tomorrow.

—John Hoyle

To write about visionary leaders is a little difficult if you have never seen one. I am fortunate because I have seen several and have been inspired by them. Historians record the lives of extraordinary visionaries who inspired people during their lives and made lasting contributions. This chapter includes the lives and influence of three visionary leaders I knew and four who have given me inspiration through their recorded words and deeds. These extraordinary individuals possessed three characteristics that best identify visionary leaders; these are (1) a profound vision of service, (2) ability to communicate the vision to others, and (3) persistence in moving toward the vision.

(VISIONARY) LEADERS I HAVE KNOWN

Mrs. Bart Shunantona

Mrs. Shunantona was my seventh-grade math teacher and school administrator in Wewoka, Oklahoma, in 1947. She was short and round and always wore bright clothes to enhance her bright Native American complexion. She was a no-nonsense teacher who literally pushed me and the other students to excel in mathematics. I was not her prize pupil—far from it! In fact, I hated math and practically everything that had to do with school. My world as a skinny seventh grader was centered on surviving football practice.

I was a sight to behold in a football uniform. I looked like an opened care package for the homeless. Call it growth spurt or whatever you like, but in the space of three summer months, I turned from an attractive, normal-sized, coordinated teacher's pet in the sixth grade (I was so smart in math that I got to dust erasers on the sidewalk once a week!) to a gangly, pimple-faced, awkward seventh grader. Changing from the best athlete to the worst in three months is a bitter pill to swallow for a kid driven by peer approval. I was competing with eighth and ninth graders to make the ninth-grade football team as an end. Coach Miller issued me a special uniform. Whereas others had close-fitting, white practice pants; a red jersey; good-looking, well-fitting cleats; and a snug-fitting helmet, I got khaki pants with sewed-in pads, a ragged white jersey that read "Property of Wewoka Junior High," shoes that were two sizes too big with loose cleats that hurt with every step, and socks that slipped to my heels. The greatest insult was an old leather helmet that was so big, every time I got hit I was looking through the ear hole!

My role as football player was blocking dummy. The first team ran a single wing offense that required four blockers to clear the way. I was placed in their way—all 6 feet 2 inches, 102 pounds of me. The shoes went one way, the helmet the other each time I stood in harm's way. After each beating, I would drag my frame home and slip in without my mother seeing the scrapes and bruises. Her response was always the same: "Well, when are you going to quit taking that abuse?" I was not about to quit and risk the ridicule of my new friends. Besides, it was all I had going for me in my life during that fall so long ago. Mrs. Shunantona was on my case for not doing my math homework and for my frequent, disruptive comments to a kid named Tommy "Lame Brain" Leamy on the next row. I was a kid who needed attention and was going about getting it my way. Mrs. Shunanona tried to reach me and appeal to my serious side, but I couldn't and wouldn't hear her. Football was on my mind.

The first game of the season was with Holdenville, and I got to suit up. My uniform was unchanged, but I was proud to be on the bench for all to see. During the first quarter, we were driving for a touchdown when Coach Miller called my name! I ran up to this god in my life and said, "Yes, Coach?" He said, "Hoyle, give your shoulder pads to Billy; his just broke." I did as ordered, but my night of pride quickly faded as I sat on the end of the bench like a plucked chicken with no future. The team continued to defeat and shut out all opponents. The day before the final game with the Shawnee Wolverines (their high school team was the Wolves), I got a red jersey with the number 9 in white on the front and back. My life was looking up because of my new identity as number 9. We were clobbering Shawnee, and everyone had played but me. With 20 seconds to go in the game, Coach Miller yelled, "Hoyle, get in there at left end." I grabbed my big helmet and must have been singing "One Moment in Time" as I raced toward the huddle. As I neared my destination, my left toe caught my right heel and the rest is a blur. My helmet went spinning across the field, and I crawled to recapture it. Just as I stood up with the helmet in place, I heard a gun fire. "Game's over," screamed the referee. I looked around toward the stands, which must have held 50,000 fans—well, at least 250. I saw Grandmother, Mother, Dad, snotty-nosed classmates who would give me grief, and my girlfriend Jean. Every person who counted in my seventh-grade life saw my defining moment on that football field that night. I was destroyed with no hope of repair. Should I run away from home or merely disappear into thin air?

The next morning, Mother woke me and told me to get ready for school. After I told her I was not going and that I was sick, she urged me, "Get up and I will iron your jeans the way you like them, and your favorite shirt is clean." I remained under the covers in my cocoon, refusing to reenter the world. After two more calls and no response, Mother brought the switch, and I got up and went to school and to Mrs. Shunantona's math class. I recall the moment I entered her classroom just as if it were yesterday. I walked in head down, watching my big feet to avoid tripping on a desk, and hurrying to find my place. Just as I was preparing to sit down, Mrs. Shunantona said, "John, you had a hard time in that football game last night, didn't you?" "Yes, ma'am," I replied. I said to myself, "Go ahead and kill me by telling the class what a failure I am." In a loud voice that still rings in my ears, she said, "Boys and girls, before we start the math lesson, listen up; I saw John Hoyle play first base on the junior police team last summer and I believe he is the best first baseman I have ever seen. Please be seated, John."

My life was saved by this leader. I was so lifted that I would have tackled calculus and trigonometry that day if Mrs. Shunantona asked me to. I became her best math student by year's end and had a new handle on my self-esteem. In two years, I made the first team in football and made my grades. Three years later, I received a full baseball scholarship to attend Texas A&M University, and I passed freshman algebra. A great leader, Mrs. Bart Shunantona had a vision of service to her students, communicated that vision through her positive words, and never gave up on any student. Her vision and the compassion to do the right thing at the right time to inspired me in that classroom in 1947. Recently, I spoke to a community college faculty colloquium and retold the story about my great teacher Mrs. Shunantona. After the presentation, a man a few years younger than I told me that he too had Mrs. Shunantona as his math teacher in Wewoka, Oklahoma. He said, "You know what? She told me the same thing about my musical talents when I was failing math!" Thus, her visionary leadership changed the lives of hundreds of her students because she knew how to touch our hearts to help us gain a vision for success in our lives.

Dr. Paul R. Hensarling

Dr. Hensarling was the visionary leader I needed at a key stage in my professional development. I was a junior-high science teacher and coach in Odessa, Texas, when I was awarded a National Science Foundation grant to attend a summer institute for science teachers at Texas A&M University in 1960. While taking science classes that summer, I was told about a dynamic professor over in education that I should meet. I did, and before our visit was over, my decision to major in educational administration was made. This man, Dr. Hensarling, was a salesman for the profession. His profound vision of service to public education, his ability to communicate that vision, and his encouragement for me to persist and complete my PhD made him a special mentor in my life and for many others aspiring doctoral students. He told me that day that "education needs people like you, John. Science is important, but people and their education are where the action will be in the next 25 years." How right he was, and the pride he wore as an educator was something I wanted.

I earned a master's in education, and Dr. Hensarling, as my committee chair, encouraged me to begin a doctorate. With his encouragement, the following summer I resigned a well-paid administrative job in Midland, Texas, and enrolled in the doctoral program at Colorado University. I struggled to prove that I belonged in the program and tried to make ends meet, and then Dr. Hensarling entered my life once more. I received a telegram inviting me to be one of six students to initiate a new doctoral program in education at Texas A&M University. He offered an assistantship of $200 per month and had arranged for my wife to interview for a teaching job in the Bryan, Texas, schools. That telegram caused me to load my wife Carolyn, son John Jr., daughter Laura Leigh, and dog Tippy into the car; pull a U-Haul trailer back to College Station, Texas; and enter the new PhD program in education at Texas A&M University for the fall semester of 1964.

Dr. Hensarling mentored me through the program, which included an appointment to teach an undergraduate class in educational psychology. He observed my teaching and made many helpful suggestions to improve my classroom effectiveness. At one point during those three long and arduous years, I thought about quitting and finding a real job because my wife had no new clothes, our car was wearing out, and my self-esteem was tumbling. When I informed Dr. Hensarling of my thoughts of quitting the program, he looked at me a moment and responded with words that remain indelible in my mind. He said, "John, you have no idea how talented you are. Remember, just be better than you think you can be." That's all he said. I stood up, shook his hand, and left his office with a resolve to live up to his words.

Paul Hensarling had a distinguished career as a teacher, coach, principal, and superintendent before becoming a professor and department head at Texas A&M University. He knew more people than any man I had met at that point in my life. He built the department of education and psychology from a four-man department to one with more than 30 members before his retirement in 1976. During his career, he was a chief architect in the creation of the College of Education and led in the creation of the doctoral program. He is remembered throughout the state of Texas for powerful speeches and practical writings to help practicing school leaders succeed in their jobs. He brought to the professorship a combination of human compassion, keen intellect, and outstanding communication skills. His former students recall Paul Hensarling as the person who had the greatest impact on their personal and professional lives. He always sought perfection in himself, and graduate students knew they could do no less.

It is perhaps impossible to identify one event or person that determined one's career and accomplishments; however, Dr. Hensarling was a powerful leader in my life. He had a vision for education and for each of his students that was compelling and exciting. During his last year, Dr. Hensarling was a recipient of the Distinguished Service Award from the American Association of School Administrators (AASA). The award was presented on February 24, 1984. He received a plaque and a book titled *A Place Called School* by John Goodlad. Dr. Hensarling gave that book to me on July 30, and he died on September 3, 1984. I had not looked at the book he gave me until several weeks after his death. I opened the front cover and found the following inscription: "For my good friend's personal library—for sharing with others—Dr. John R. Hoyle, who over a lifetime has done more for me than anyone else, professionally and personally. There is no way to repay such deeds—they are part of the nature of John Hoyle. Sincerely, Paul R. Hensarling." I cried as I read those words because he once again challenged me to try to "be better than you think you can be." Dr. Hensarling's service vision for public education and his graduate students, his extraordinary skills in communicating that vision, and his persistence toward accomplishing the vision placed him at the top of the visionary leadership list.

Dr. Paul B. Salmon

Dr. Salmon, former executive director of the AASA, is a third leader I have known and a name more widely known in education. Dr. Salmon served with distinction as executive director of AASA from 1971 until May 1985. A graduate of Whittier College, he had majors in elementary education and history and was an outstanding football player. After graduation, he taught seventh grade in Whittier, California, and then joined the U.S. Navy during World War II. His exceptional leadership capacities were identified early in his education career when he moved from a classroom teaching post to superintendent of Bloomfield School District in Artesia, California. After serving as superintendent of schools in Covina-Valley Unified School District, he moved to Pasadena, California, and then on to Sacramento in 1968. His selection as AASA executive director in 1971 placed him in the national spotlight in education. During the next 16 years, Paul was in the forefront of educational reform efforts nationwide and became the spokesperson for school leaders around the world in the areas of school organization and leadership. He was highly visible on Capitol Hill when education legislation and child welfare issues were under review. His commanding presence around legislators came from both his physical size—he stood 6 feet 3 inches and weighed 250 pounds—and his booming and articulate voice. He was in demand to appear on the *Today Show*, the *MacNeil/Lehrer NewsHour*, and Public Broadcasting's *Late Night*, and he made many appearances on local television programs discussing current problems of education. Among his honors was the honorary Doctor of Humane Letters from Whittier College in 1984. He was a distinguished professor of the National Academy for School Executives and was a frequent writer for news outlets and for major journals in education.

He traveled the country, working with school administrators and giving keynote speeches in all 50 states and around the world. His high energy and enthusiasm for public education lifted spirits and provided needed advice for school boards and superintendents engaged in school improvement. His belief in building collaboration between practitioners and professors led to several lasting changes in the preparation and practice of school leaders. He initiated the Higher Education Advisory Committee, composed of AASA members who were in professorships or university administrative positions. The committee created programs that have had a major impact on research and best practice in American education. One product of the committee is the AASA award for professor of the year, which includes a stipend for a respected professor to spend three months in Arlington, Virginia, at AASA headquarters as a scholar in residence. I was selected for the award in 1982, and during my first two weeks in Arlington Dr. Salmon asked me to facilitate a project to develop a set of guidelines for the preparation of school administrators. The guidelines were completed in October 1982 and became the first national benchmarks for the preparation and professional development of principals and superintendents. The guidelines led to the publication of a widely used textbook, *Skills for Successful School Leaders* (Hoyle, English, & Steffy, 1985). The second edition was completed in 1990 and revised in 1994, and the most recent edition, titled *Skills for Successful 21st Century*

School Leaders, appeared in 1998. Other projects that Paul Salmon inspired included a program that provided recognition for outstanding university preparation programs and additional activities to bring university and public school leaders together.

The attribute that set Paul Salmon on a special level, and the reason that he is described in this book, is that he always asked administrators, project directors, and others if children would truly benefit from their plans and projects. In 1982, when Paul charged me to write the guidelines, I spent many long nights conducting research and writing. Each morning, Paul would scrutinize the draft, look up under bushy eyebrows, and ask, "Where are the kids in this?" Back I went to rewrite what I thought was already a masterpiece. After several rejections of portions of the manuscript, he declared it fit for submission to the AASA executive committee for their review and approval. Students and their needs are prominent in each of the skills and competencies in the document. In fact, since 1982, whenever I begin a class or an invited lecture around the nation, I draw a round face, include eyes and a big smile, and label it the "generic kid."

Completed in 1982, the guidelines became a guide for the majority of the education leadership preparation programs in the United States. The eight skill areas in the guidelines were the foundation for the Professional Standards for the Superintendency published by AASA in 1993. These 1982 guidelines and the 1993 Professional Standards for the Superintendency become the benchmarks for later standards developed by other school administrator groups, including those widely used today by the Interstate School Leaders Licensure Consortium (ISLLC) and the National Council for the Accreditation of Colleges of Education (NCATE).

Paul B. Salmon retired from AASA on March 31, 1985, and began a speaking and consulting career to share his vision and energy across America. His life and exciting career were cut short by a Delta Airline disaster in Dallas, Texas, on July 16, 1985. This accident was a tragedy not only for Paul's family and friends but for education as well. His dynamic personality, powerful persuasive voice, and tireless energy could not be replaced. However, his legacy lives on in the students he taught, the administrators he prepared, the education legislation he influenced, and the positive image he maintained for those around him. Paul Salmon had a service vision for America's schools and communicated that vision to thousands, including me, and he remained focused on his vision his entire professional career. He exemplified the characteristics of outstanding leaders found in the leadership research and in the conversations about the mystique of those we want to follow.

What They Had in Common

These leaders I knew and respected. Each of the three—Mrs. Shunantona, Dr. Hensarling, and Dr. Salmon—was a unique leader with many winning attributes. Two were not national figures; one was. One was a Native American teacher in a small Oklahoma town, one was a professor in a major university, and one directed a national professional administrators' association with over 18,000 members. What, then, were the common leadership characteristics that marked their journey through my life? Three characteristics come to mind: profound vision of service, clear communication, and a commitment to persist.

They were all very active servant leaders and busy people with limited time to spare, but they found the time for me. I could have left Mrs. Shunantona's life with a hatred for math and for teachers in general, but she had a vision for me and her other students. Paul Hensarling could have ignored my whining as just a stage of graduate school, but he listened and used the right words at the right time to keep me moving toward my goal. Paul Salmon, in his lofty position, could have been too busy to ask me to attempt to develop a set of preparation guidelines or to critique each line looking for the "kids." The capacity to care for me and hundreds of others is the first ingredient of the makeup of these three idols of mine.

There was never any need to hire an interpreter to explain anything my three leaders said. Mrs. Shunantona communicated the right words and expressions to build a fire in me to succeed. Paul Hensarling's words were filled with hope; they were positive and challenging as he spoke them or wrote them in professional journals. His penmanship was an art form, and his words, even those spoken in a whisper in his last few days, were as clear as a late summer sky. Paul Salmon was a master with a phrase and didn't mind correcting me if he detected an improper use of a word. He once nailed me for using "irregardless" and another person for using "hopefully" in the wrong way. He believed that the words a person used were the window to his or her character. The correct word in the right place at the right time from these leaders left an indelible impression on me and others.

These three leaders never gave up. Mrs. Shunantona refused to let me or any other student give up. Failure was not in her vocabulary when it came to her students. She spent more than 40 years telling the same story to all of her students and their parents. She left in me a drive to finish what I start. Dr. Hensarling was a master at making the routine of starting the same class each semester or planning the annual superintendent conference appear to be fresh and exciting. He never tired of doing the same things because he updated the content of his classes each semester and the conference program each year based on the realities of the time. Also, his extraordinary ability to listen to the woes of burned-out graduate students and faculty, and then select the right words to give them a renewed spirit, were marks of a gifted leader. Dr. Salmon was a bulldog at seeing a job through to completion. He could hold his own with the most persuasive politician on Capitol Hill or with critics of public schools. He believed that persistence loaded with good data could win most battles for education and the children of America's schools. Dr. Salmon was the one person educators wanted on their side in a debate on any educational policy matter. You knew he would never cut and run when the battle began.

Thus the visionary attributes of a service vision to help others, the ability to communicate the vision of hope through words and deeds with clear meaning, and a commitment to persist toward goal accomplishment defined these three great leaders. You, the reader, can no doubt select visionary leaders from your past who also possess these and other attributes. Although the literature on leadership is teeming with lists of attributes and characteristics of leaders, it is important to remember those who didn't need a list to guide them in the complex roles they played as leaders. These real people, facing real-world problems with visions for a better world and sharing that vision with many others, ran the complete race of leadership. Throughout the remainder of this book, I will refer to the three leaders that I knew and to the four great leaders of history that I did not know but wish I had.

LEADERS I WISH I HAD KNOWN

The following leaders of history have intrigued me for many years. I have often wondered what it would have been like to have engaged these giants in conversation about leadership and the skills they each used to inspire ordinary people to extraordinary accomplishments. I have chosen Jesus of Nazareth, Joan of Arc, Winston Churchill, and a young American military hero named Sean Sims as the leaders I would like to have known.

Jesus of Nazareth

Jesus is certainly a well-known figure. The written accounts of his leadership accomplishments are found in the four Gospels of Matthew, Mark, Luke, and John and in the Epistles of the New Testament. Even though the facts of Jesus's career are subject to question, and many traditional sayings ascribed to Jesus are unreliable, his larger-than-life influence has had a major impact on the course of human history. Very little is known about his childhood and youth in terms of formal education. The scriptures recorded his baptism by his cousin John the Baptist and his time of meditation and solitude before beginning a three-year ministry. This three-year ministry included profound teachings using the language of the common people of the day. He reached out to the oppressed, to children, and to the ill and outcast of society. The scriptures tell of miracle cures and revolutionary ideas that caught the eyes of the Pharisees and scribes. This ruling clique decided to eliminate Jesus, whom they considered a revolutionary leader and violent reformer. He was arrested, convicted of crimes carrying the death penalty in Jewish law, and turned over to the Romans to carry out the sentence. He was charged with treason against Rome, and the Roman procurator Pontius Pilate delivered Jesus to be crucified. According to the scriptures, three days after his crucifixion an angel told visitors to his grave that he had risen from the dead. Later, he was seen by his disciples before ascending into heaven.

Writers, artists, musicians, and others have long been inspired by the incidents in the life of Jesus. Brooks (1954) wrote about the leadership of Jesus, saying,

He never traveled more than 200 miles from home, never wrote a book, never earned a college degree, but all of the governments that ever sat, all of the armies that ever marched, all the navies that ever sailed and all the kings who ever sat have not had the impact on history as this single, solitary life. (p. 45)

Jesus of Nazareth also displayed the three characteristics of the three visionary leaders I knew personally. He had a deep and profound vision of service to others, especially those unable to help themselves. He used the common language of the day and used parables to communicate clear visions of hope and caring to all who listened. His message was so clear and persuasive that individuals dropped what they were doing and followed Him. Clearly, Jesus had a commitment to persist to accomplish his vision even unto death. He died for his cause, which was to lift the human race to become one of compassion and equity for all races and creeds.[1]

Joan of Arc

Joan of Arc is a French saint and national heroine who, through her visions, charisma, and determination, almost succeeded in chasing English forces from French soil. Born in Domremy, France, in 1412, she began to hear the voices of three saints from which she drew her vision early in her life in her garden in Domremy. Inspired by these voices, Joan of Arc convinced the authorities that she could serve her nation, lead troops, and win in battle to lift the siege of Orleans and conquer other English-held encampments along the Loire River. She then convinced Charles VII to march on Rheims, where he was crowned in her presence. However, King Charles and his close advisors slowed the military progress of Joan and her armies by negotiating with the duke of Burgundy, England's independent ally, whose forces later captured her at the battle of Compiegne and sold her to the English.

Her trial in Rouen was an effort to force her to recant the voices that convinced her to place her faith in God over the church hierarchy and to end her quest to lead soldiers in battle against the English. She refused and was condemned for heresy and sorcery. In 1431, she was burned at the stake. A later trial in 1456 reversed the decision and praised her for inspiring her country in a time of English conquest. She was canonized as a saint in 1920.

Historians are in general agreement about the visionary servant leadership style of Joan of Arc. She was inspired by her faith to lead in battle, and she led with spear in hand without a helmet for protection to enable her soldiers to see her long blonde hair. At the siege of Orleans, she was severely wounded in the shoulder by a spear. She was assisted in removing the spear and cried out "Vive [long live] la France" to rally her men to continue the battle. This display of bravery to serve others, to communicate visions of hope, and to persist during perilous times inspired them to continue fighting and to take Orleans. Her capacity of service and caring for her beloved France and her people led Joan of Arc to convince the Dauphin and others at Chinon to give her an army. She was a master communicator to her superiors, to soldiers, and to the people of France to persuade them to follow her in this noble cause. Her commitment to persist against the English-controlled court of law that conducted her irregular and biased trial and to stay true to her beliefs in the face of death is a testimony to her values of truth and determination. The judge for the trial was an ambitious bishop named Pierre Cauchon who was a pawn of the English and conducted a trial that was later found to be an injustice. In 1456, Pope Calixtus III declared Joan's name forever cleansed of all charges against it (Banfield, 1985). Joan was canonized in 1920 and is known as the patron saint of France.

Her visionary leadership has been an inspiration for some of the world's artists, military leaders, and writers. Banfield said,

Thousands of people still turn to Joan's story about inspired vision, from the soldier of whom great bravery is required to the young girl who needs the quiet courage to be honest with her lover. In this brief but so-powerful life they find the help they need to remain true, through whatever arises, to the voice within them. (1985, p. 107)[2]

Winston Churchill

Winston Churchill was one of the most revered statesmen, military strategists, orators, and charismatic leaders of the twentieth century. He inspired his compatriots to fight on against tremendous odds in World War II. Born into nobility and wealth, Churchill was a problem child and poor student. He lived a checkered childhood full of mischief, school failure, and heartache for his parents, who were too busy to give him a happy home and childhood. Churchill spent the rest of his life trying to make his father proud of him.

After a lackluster record in several schools, he entered the Royal Military Academy at Sandhurst, where he became a serious student of literature and military science. At age 16, he revealed his visionary prowess when he went to see the family doctor about a speech impediment—a slight lisp. The doctor told him to forget about the lisp because as a soldier, he would not be a speaker but a fighter. Churchill's personal vision led him to believe that he would some-day become a great statesman like his father and that "I must be able to make an important speech without worrying that I cannot say the letter 's'" (Rogers, 1986, p. 25). His powerful, persuasive speeches became his trademark as a leader. He started his path to power by becoming a war correspondent and soldier to gain fame and recog-nition so that he could enter public office like his father. His writings caught the public's attention early. His first book, about a war against the native tribesmen of India titled *The Story of the Malakand Field Force,* was widely read and was the first of many volumes on war, politics, and his life. After escaping from the enemy during the Boer War, Churchill became a national celebrity. This fame led to his elec-tion to Parliament and to more than 50 years of public service to his country.

He met both success and failure during his long and storied career. However, he continued to communicate hope and persisted toward his vision of leadership for England and his people. During World War I, he was forced to resign as first lord of the admiralty because of the decisions he made that led indirectly to the disaster at Gallipoli. He lost his seat in Parliament in 1921 but was reelected in 1924. His vision called him to warn the world about the increasing aggression of the new German leader, Adolf Hitler, in 1932, but he had few listeners until it was almost too late. Appointed prime min-ister a year after Britain declared war against Germany, he became a man of destiny for his country. After his appointment, his vision-ary, inspiring words before the House of Commons became among his most famous: "I have nothing to offer but blood, toil, tears, and sweat; you ask what is our aim? I can answer in one word: victory—victory in spite of all terror" (Rogers, 1986, p. 75). Later, during one of the darkest hours of the war, he galvanized his people when he said, "We shall not flag or fail. We shall go the end. We shall fight in France, we shall fight on the seas and oceans, we shall fight with growing confidence and growing strength in the air, we shall defend our island whatever the cost may be" (Rogers, 1986, p. 77). He was a master with words at the right time throughout his career. Speaking before the House of Commons on June 18, 1940, Churchill said, "Let us therefore brace ourselves, that if the British Empire and its Commonwealth last for a thousand years, men will still say, 'This was their finest hour'" (Rogers, 1986, p. 75).

But he was also known for his biting wit. A story is told about Churchill and Lady Astor, a very dignified lady of wealth, sitting next to each other at a dinner party. She said, "Winston, if I were your wife, I'd poison your soup." He replied, "Nancy, if I were your husband, I'd drink it" (Manchester, 1983, p. 34). Another, undocumented story is told about an interaction at a formal banquet with Churchill sitting across the table from Lady Astor. After he finished off a bottle of red wine, Lady Astor said, "Why Winston, you are drunk!" Churchill responded, "Yes my lady, and you are ugly. Furthermore, in the morning, I shall be sober and you'll still be ugly!"

While Churchill sometimes spoke with an acid tongue, he was quite loquacious and tenacious. He continued when lesser persons would have changed careers. After inspiring the British people and the world to help defeat the German and Italian forces, his party lost in the elections of 1945, and he lost his post as prime minister because the people wanted to go in a new, more liberal direction. He continued his speaking and writing and positive approach, and he returned to office as prime minister following the Conservative election victory in 1951. Dubbed Knight of the Garter by Queen Elizabeth II in 1953, he later won the Nobel Prize for literature. A master of the quip, during his final year of life he said, "I'm ready to meet my maker; whether my maker is prepared for the great ordeal of meeting me is another matter" (Rogers, 1986, p. 107). A visionary and humorist to the end, Winston Churchill was a great man for his time and for his beloved England (Rogers, 1986).

Churchill clearly exemplifies my three characteristics for visionary leaders. He had a profound vision of service for his country and the world, and he communicated it superbly in his inspiring radio messages that brought hope to his country during the Nazi blitzkrieg destruction of London and other English cities. His commitment to persist was symbolized by his words, "We shall not flag or fail. We shall go to the end." His love for the people of his country in peace and war marked his life, and his speeches and writing are among the most long remembered. His "victory in spite of all terror" speech sums up his commitment to persist when others had given up. His vision was toward a better day for England and the price it took to gain it.[3]

Sean Sims

The final visionary leader I wish I had known is U.S. Army Captain Sean Sims, who died in action while clearing insurgents from homes in Fallujah, Iraq, on November 13, 2004. Sean, a 1996 graduate of Texas A&M University and member of the First Infantry Division, stationed in Germany, had been assigned to Iraq for 10 months and was set to return home in February 2005. The handsome young Sean, with a strong jaw and unassuming smile, excelled as a member of Texas A&M University's Corps of Cadets, becoming company commander of his company, L-2. Sean was a member of the famed Ross Volunteers, an elite unit within the Corps. He also participated in the Ranger Challenge, a physically demanding competition in infantry tactics.

Patrick Seiber, a friend who attended Texas A&M University with Sims, said, "When you think of what an Aggie cadet should be, it was Sean Sims. He was a go-to guy and true leader in every sense of the word. He'd give you a straight answer. Calm under pressure." Sean's father, Thomas "Reb" Sims, a retired army colonel, said, "He led his troops from the front and was proud of his missions searching for insurgents and helping to bring peace to Iraq. He wasn't a John Wayne kind of leader. He was a quiet and thoughtful leader who would speak quietly and his men would just respond. I think they respected him because they realized he didn't have an agenda—he was only concerned with their welfare." According to Corps of Cadets buddy Mark Stodola, "Sean saw much in the faces of the Iraq people, some of whom he knew had to be dealt with violently, but most of whom he loved helping."

Sean's vision for service to his country and to the people of Iraq and his hope for a better life for others was demonstrated by both words and deeds, and his persistence toward his vision of peace in Iraq was profound. On the day he was killed in battle, an Iraqi translator befriended by Sims had to be held back from charging into a building through a hail of bullets to save him. Sims's friend Mark said, "Sean was never boastful, though he had every right to be. He accepted everyone's basic goodness and equality. Simply being his friend has made me bolder and less prideful. I am a better person today because this boy I met 14 years ago showed me what a man can be." Sean's father said, "He had so much to live for, but he accepted that risk like the other young men and women who are over there, who are all making that sacrifice so that we can be free" (Huffman, 2004).

I never had the opportunity to meet and visit with Sean Sims while he was a student leader at Texas A&M University or during his time as a military officer. That is my loss. Sean was a hero and a great American who gave his full measure of devotion and love for his nation and for peace-seeking people in Iraq. War is hell, and Sean Sims, a model visionary leader, can never be replaced. However, in future years when young Iraqi boys and girls live in a free and democratic country, they will remember the price that Sean Sims and other brave warriors paid and the servant leadership he shared to make the world a better place for us all.[4]

CONCLUSIONS

These seven leaders—three of whom I knew and four I wish I had known—are the inspiration and context of this book about leadership and visioning. Each of these special personalities moved people and programs to success. By their character, wisdom, and vision, they led others to find their own inner greatness. Arthur M. Schlesinger Jr. captured the essence of the influence of great leaders when he wrote, "The signal benefit the great leaders confer is to embolden the rest of us to live according to our own best selves, to be active, insistent, and resolute in affirming our own sense of things. . . . And they attest to the wisdom and power that may lie within the most unlikely of us" (Rogers, 1986, p. 9).

While conducting research on visioning leadership, I revisited the lives and accomplishments of several prominent leaders other than those seven I selected for this chapter. Among them were Mahatma Gandhi, John F. Kennedy Jr., Martin Luther King Jr., Florence Nightingale, Mary McLeod Bethune, Abraham Lincoln, Audie Murphy, Cesar Chavez and his helper Dolores Huerta, and Christa McAuliffe. These remarkable leaders were unique personalities who could inspire the rest of us to live according to our own highest ideals. Out of their uniqueness came a consistent set of characteristics or leadership attributes that provide help for others who wish to become visionary leaders.

In the following four chapters, the reader will be reminded of these great leaders and the attributes they possessed. I hope that you, the reader, will recall great leaders in your life and reflect how their influence on you has challenged you as Dr. Hensarling did me with his words, "Be better than you think you can be."

NOTES

1. Details in the life of Jesus were selected from the *Columbia Viking Desk Encyclopedia* (New York: Viking, 1953).

2. The primary source for the life of Joan of Arc was *Joan of Arc* by S. Banfield (New York: Chelsea House, 1985).

3. The primary source for the life of Winston Churchill was *Winston Churchill* by J. Rogers (New York: Chelsea House, 1986).

4. The primary source for the Sean Sims story was an article by H. Huffman in *The Bryan–College Station Eagle,* November 28, 2004.

CHAPTER THREE

Motivating Others to Engage in Futuring

W hat motivates individuals to overcome adversity and rise to great heights? Why did Hazel Brannen Smith continue her fight for justice when faced with hatred and violence from racists in her own home town? Hazel Brannen Smith, a journalist, fulfilled a vision to return to her hometown in rural Mississippi in 1954 and start a newspaper that would take a different direction in editorial writing. She began writing editorials about healing the relationships between black and white people and encouraging people to work together to improve schools and the community. She suggested that this would help the town prosper and offer brighter futures for their children. However, Hazel Smith had forgotten how deeply rooted racial hatred was among certain individuals. She received physical threats from business owners, who pulled their advertising dollars from her paper. Lifelong friends ostracized her, her husband died in a tragic accident, and her newspaper building was burned to the ground. This small dynamo of a woman held on to her vision, and a handful of loyal employees remained by her side while she went elsewhere to borrow money to reopen her newspaper. Another newspaper was begun in an attempt to thwart her efforts to resurrect her paper and to solicit the local advertising dollar. Undaunted, Hazel Brannen Smith reopened the paper and continued her editorial writing. Her work began to open some closed minds and the community grew more accepting of her words of reconciliation. Her persistence inspired the community to become more inclusive of African Americans in educational and community programs. Her courage and drive to turn a vision into a reality led to national recognition. In 1964 Hazel Brannen Smith became the first woman to win a Pulitzer Prize for editorial writing. Her inspired vision of service, her ability to clearly describe the vision, and her refusal to give up made her community a better place.

EXTRINSIC AND INTRINSIC MOTIVATION

What was the source of motivation for Hazel Smith to overcome seemingly insurmountable odds? Why do some individuals thrive on creating something new and better? It is true that great visionary leaders have a knack for inventing their own future. However, they understand motivation theories and why others are motivated to accept a vision as their own. Motivation theorists agree that motivation can be divided into two broad categories—extrinsic and intrinsic. Extrinsic motivation theory is derived from the work of Thorndike (1911) and Hull (1943), which is centered on the idea that the link between a stimulus and response is strengthened when it is followed by a satisfactory outcome. Skinner (1974) demonstrated that the use of positive reinforcement would increase the probability that a behavior would be repeated. Thus, when workers or students are given praise or good grades contingent on good performance, they will continue striving to receive the recognition. If, on the other hand, the workers or students perform below expectations, negative reinforcement is used (low grades, loss of privileges, etc.)

But a visionary leader cannot rely simply on extrinsic motivation when persuading others to share his or her vision. Leaders must rely in addition on meeting the intrinsic needs of individuals; these include needs for pride in the job itself, a sense of achievement, and recognition for a job well done. These rewards and positive outcomes accrue to those who have been personally involved in creating a vision statement and its purpose; they may not be as evident to others.

The most important element in the visioning process for any organization is the enthusiasm and vision of the formal leader. If the leader envisions greater production in a business or school, then he or she must communicate the vision and plans to others and hope the vision is viewed as intrinsically motivating. Intrinsic motivation is based on the theory that individuals are inherently motivated to excel, and that they derive personal satisfaction from their accomplishments and being a part of an exciting organization. That is, individuals need leaders who can help them find an intrinsic drive to excel. This drive can include a service vision and a cause beyond themselves. This was very evident when a few loyal employees stood with Hazel Smith in rebuilding the newspaper.

According to DeCharms (1984), individuals believe that they alone are the cause of their own behavior and they choose to engage in projects for personal satisfaction rather than gaining a reward or to please another person. Another motivation theorist (Maslow, 1954) simply claims that one individual cannot actually motivate another since motivation is not a form of behavior. Instead, according to Maslow, motivation comes from within in the form of a need, drive, urge, idea, or motive. Classroom practices from preschool to graduate studies that stress such intrinsic motivation include (1) making tasks moderately difficult; (2) varying the format and nature of classroom assignments; (3) encouraging the notion of self-determination by allowing the learner a choice of tasks; (4) encouraging students to shape assignments that will engage them, be personally meaningful, and provide enjoyment; (5) emphasizing the value of information rather than rewards as the driving force for learning; and (6) enhancing students' feelings of mastery and competence (Stipek, 1996, as cited in Hoyle, Bjork, Collier, & Glass, 2005). Motivation to accomplish great things begins with the internal drive to succeed regardless of the obstacles.

Goal Theory

Perhaps the most intriguing intrinsic motivation theory is goal theory (Locke & Latham, 1990). Locke and Latham base their theory on the premise that difficult goals are more motivational than moderate or easy ones, specific goals are more motivational that general ones, and goals established by mutual agreement of the worker and supervisor tend to produce greater performance than those established by either party.

A former Baylor University football coach, Grant Teaff, tells a story about the magic of goal theory and its motivational power (personal communication, April 14, 1995). During the first day on the job, Teaff was under the stadium clearing out old equipment when several of his players walked by. Teaff introduced himself to each one. He extended his hand to one tall, slender, shy young man and said, "Hi, I am Grant Teaff, your new football coach. What is your name?" Unknown to Teaff the young man had a speech impediment or stutter and could not provide his name to Teaff. Embarrassed, the young man walked away. Teaff asked one of his assistants about the young man, and the assistant's response was, "Oh, don't worry about him, coach; he is the fourth-string quarterback, and the way he stutters, he will get somebody killed at the line of scrimmage trying to call signals." Grant Teaff did not forget about this young man.

Part of Teaff's plan to build a winning tradition was to ask his players to write down their personal goals and team goals at the beginning of spring training. In the spring of 1972, this skinny sophomore came in with his written goals and handed them to Teaff. The young athlete then tried to orally repeat the goals, but the stutter made for a prolonged report. Teaff then asked to see the list. It read, "I want to quarterback the Baylor Bears to the first Southwest Conference championship in more than 50 years and lead the team to the Cotton Bowl; I want to be a top student and study for the ministry, and next I want to be a youth pastor in a large church in the Dallas–Fort Worth area." After a brief pause while looking into the intense eyes of the young man, Teaff said, "Son, what can I do to help your dreams come true by accomplishing these goals?" The coach could have told him, "Sorry, son, but you and I know you can't reach your goal as a quarterback with that speech problem."

During the quarterback's first season, he was a backup and played little. When he called a play in the huddle, a big tackle would reach over and slap the quarterback's thigh pad, and then he could call the play without stuttering; in his junior year, he claims that he frequently sang the signals to avoid stuttering. His senior year, Neal Jeffrey clearly called the signals himself and led the Baylor Bears to their first Southwest Conference championship in over 50 years. This 1974 team and its visionary quarterback became known as the "miracle on the Brazos." Neal was an excellent student and finished seminary. He is currently minister in one of the largest Baptist churches in the Dallas, Texas area and is in demand as a motivational speaker for youth conventions and rallies. Goals can be a powerful motivating force for individuals in all walks of life.

MOTIVATE THE HEART

Visionary leaders tell stories and persuade others to consider ideas that can bring positive changes in the system that can benefit them personally and improve lives and communities. Most professionals are sick and tired of appeasing the U.S. Office of Education, state departments of education, and bosses who talk about a new gee-whiz reform strategy with little or no input by those forced to implement the new plan. In education and other government agencies people have been bombarded with movements and fads such as quality circles, strategic planning, effective schools, total quality management, brain-based learning, curriculum alignment, and miracle software packages that can turn struggling students into Nobel laureates in six weeks. Teachers and administrators have been assigned to groups to dream dreams, create belief statements, plan curricula, and develop staff only to be told six months later to forget the last plan and launch a new one. When organizational leaders bemoan that "my staff is belligerent when faced with a new plan," it is a clear indication that no foundation for collaboration was built and the trust level is zero.

What can a leader do to make his or her personal vision become a shared group vision? Fredrick Herzberg (1968) and other motivation theorists found that two of the most powerful satisfiers for people are personal achievement and personal recognition. These two satisfiers (motivators) appear to be far more important than the supervisors, the work plan, interpersonal relationships, or policies. That is, if workers, such as teachers, engineers, bankers, or construction workers, hold the belief that the work they do is beneficial to others; if they believe that they perform their work at high levels; and if they receive recognition in the form of praise from supervision, peers, and customers; then they have a sense of purpose in life. Buckingham and Coffman (1999) listed the four questions asked most frequently by employees in most organizations as follows:

1. Do I have the opportunity to do what I do best each day on the job?

2. Am I provided the necessary materials and training to successfully do my job each day?

3. In the last two weeks has my supervisor given me praise for doing a good job?

4. Does someone at work care about me as a person? (p. 34)

According to Buckingham and Coffman, if members of an organization can answer yes to these four questions, then the chances of high performance and high morale are good.

Thus, if a leader's vision is to become shared, the vision must meet each person's intrinsic need to reach for higher performance and to gain a feeling of personal accomplishment for the good of others. While a personal vision is the most powerful for individual accomplishment, it holds little potential for becoming a corporate vision unless it is embraced in the organization. For example, John Kennedy's vision to land a man on the moon within a decade became shared by others. Millions of dollars were appropriated by Congress, NASA selected and trained the astronauts, and the nation focused on making the vision happen. A failed example is that of the Edison Schools organization, which had a dream to create 1,000 Edison schools by 1999 to compete with public schools. This dream failed to materialize because the vision was shared only among a small elite group who failed to communicate why the for-profit venture was in the best interests of American education and its democratic purpose of public schools for all children. These venture capitalists did not fully understand that most Americans did not support the Edison vision of using public funds for personal and corporate gain. The free enterprise vision of Edison and other for-profit efforts has never fully caught on in urban schools, where school funding remains inadequate to ensure equal opportunity for all children. People must be included in the vision building process and have a collective sense of ownership about how the vision affects their careers and personal lives.

Visionary leaders, according to futurist Joel Barker, literally experience their victories or accomplishments in their minds long before they actually occur. Thus, these leaders rely on their service vision, their ability to communicate the vision, and their ability to persist until the vision is embraced by others in the organization. In order to bring greater accuracy to visioning and forecasting, the futurist community in recent years has developed more sophisticated research methods and techniques and some see the possibility of a genuine science of the future—not a natural science like chemistry or biology, but a social science like sociology or anthropology (Cornish, 2004).

MOTIVATION AND THE ART OF PERSUASION

After creating a vision, administrators and managers need the skill of persuasion. Without this skill, many visions and great dreams go unrealized because of lack of support from others in the organization. Management and leadership scholars concur on one basic truth—cooperation cannot be forced! Thus, the art of persuasion becomes a most critical skill in building collaborative teams. According to George Manners and Joseph Steger (1979), persuasion is difficult to teach or learn. Of the nine leadership skills and management skills they identify, persuasion is the most difficult skill to master. Most administrators do not think themselves to be persuasive and able to inspire others. Also, some see persuasion as an act of power by allocating or manipulating symbolic coercion or rewards to get people to go along with the vision (Rebore, 2003).

In spite of mixed perceptions of the meaning and use of persuasion, it is vital if teams are to be successful in any endeavor. Persuasion enables the leader to get people to do things contrary to their own wishes or desires. Leaders must be able to convince others—often those over whom they have no administrative control—to follow them in a project or idea. When speaking to a group or a large gathering, leaders must get them personally involved by touching their emotions. They must create in their listeners a desire to be a part of a cause beyond themselves. I was a junior-high school administrator when I heard President John F. Kennedy say, "Ask not what your country can do for you; ask what you can do for your country." This statement plus the shock of his tragic assassination led me to pursue a PhD and strive to make a difference for others. Great leaders like John Kennedy and Martin Luther King Jr. are remembered for their vision and their ability to convince others, through the art of persuasion, to join in making a vision happen. Visionary leaders are remembered for their ability to touch the hearts of individuals to turn their minds toward great accomplishments.

Scott Cutlip, Allen Center, and Glen Broom (1985), authorities on the art and science of persuasion, offer four research-based principles for using persuasion:

1. Identification Principle. Most people will ignore an idea or point of view unless they see that it affects their personal fears, desires, hopes, or aspirations.

2. Action Principle. People seldom buy ideas separated from action—either action taken by the sponsor of the idea or action that the people themselves can conveniently take to prove the merit of the idea.

3. Familiarity and Trust Principle. People buy ideas only from those they trust; they are influenced by, or adopt, only those opinions or points of view put forward by individuals, corporations, or institutions that they regard as credible.

4. Clarity Principle. The situation must be clear, not confusing. The thing people observe, read, see, or hear—the thing that produces their impressions—must be clear, not subject to several interpretations. People tend to see things as black or white. To communicate, leaders must employ words, symbols, or stereotypes that the receiver comprehends and responds to. (pp. 178–179)

If people view you as a person who has the knowledge and skills they need to grow as professionals and who can lead them in a plan for action that is both credible and clearly understood, then you are mastering the art of persuasion. President Lyndon Johnson was a master of persuasion when he persuaded Congress to pass legislation and provide the funding for the War on Poverty. A school principal or superintendent who declares that "all students will learn at a high level" must follow up the statement with intensive professional development and denounce excuses by teachers and others who claim that children from poverty and certain ethnic groups cannot learn at high levels. Father Hesburgh, former president of the University of Notre Dame, believed that in order to persuade others you must have a clear vision and communicate the vision in clear words. He said, "You can't blow an uncertain trumpet!"

CONCLUSIONS

Motivation is not a measurable behavior, but an intrinsic need or drive to act. This drive can be toward creating a better world or destroying the world. Visionary leaders with the intrinsic drive to create better organizations that meet the needs of others become the leaders of industry, government, education, and athletics. Leaders who seek to improve their visioning and motivation skills can learn valuable lessons from the visionaries of history. In Chapter 2, I described how Joan of Arc had a vision to chase the British from French soil. Galileo's visions and astronomical discoveries confirmed Copernicus's theory of the solar system, and even though he was forced by church authorities to recant his findings, his vision inspired others to change astronomy forever. John F. Kennedy Jr.'s vision led Neil Armstrong to step on the moon and exclaim, "That's one small step for man, one giant leap for mankind." Unfortunately, Kennedy didn't live to see his vision happen. Adolph Hitler had a vision of a "thousand-year reign" that led to the extermination of six million people and the destruction of Nazi Germany and most of Europe. Thus visionary leadership has been used for both good and evil.

Futuring requires skills in persuading others to collaborate in meeting new challenges and creating a better world. If the leader is excited about creating new opportunities for all learners in a school or university, then that excitement must be shared by others. If a new product or process is to become a best seller, then the entire organization must be persuaded to begin marketing and production. People in the organization must view the vision as personal, see how the vision can become a reality, trust the leader, and clearly understand the steps required to make the vision happen. Motivation is complicated, but it is vital to success in any endeavor. Moving from good to great requires a team with one vision and hearts beating together to accomplish the common good.

CHAPTER FOUR

Making Visions Happen

I f your service vision has been communicated in a persuasive manner, and you have involved others in the vision and the processes of making the vision happen, your chance of success as a visionary leader is probable. Ralph Waldo Emerson believed in dreamers who dream big ideas, but also that these ideas must be fulfilled. Some administrators must talk about every idea for so long that they squeeze the life out of the idea. Unless the leader has the skill to capture the imagination of a group in a short time, the idea or vision will die quickly. Busy professionals protect their time, and unless their intellect and soul can be reached in a few moments, they are out of here. If the group feels the fire in an idea and if the idea or vision is focused on each of them and their role in it, the vision is alive. The leader must breathe life into his or her vision (Kouzes & Posner, 1987). The coals of an idea must be blown into a bright flame by those who will make the vision come to pass.

An idea that grew from the battlefield of Southeast Asia led to a national symbol of bravery and loyalty. In 1969, a young soldier was severely wounded by a mortar shell in Vietnam, and several of his buddies were killed or wounded. The young soldier, Jan Scruggs, was in and out of hospitals for three years to repair his broken body and spirit. He endured sleepless nights because of the memories of his friends who died in that far-off hellhole in Southeast Asia. Also, he was distressed that America had forgotten the price his friends had paid for their country in a controversial war, and because he didn't want the American public to forget his buddies, he decided to do something about it. He had no money and little influence to create a memorial or a fund, so he and two friends contacted members of Congress about the idea and then spent their own money to create the Vietnam Memorial Fund. Scruggs called a news conference to announce the fund. Next, Congress set aside a piece of land near the Lincoln Memorial in Washington, DC, and gave Jan and his committee five years to raise the funds for the memorial. The appeal for funding caught the attention of the public, and the money was raised in two years. On November 12, 1982, Jan Scruggs and his buddies and friends participated in the dedication of the beautiful Vietnam Veterans Memorial. Jan Scruggs had a vision to honor young American soldiers who gave their full measure of devotion for their country. One person, one vision, and a determination to tell an important story created a symbol of respect and beauty dedicated to his fallen friends. His persistence and the determination to enlist others caused the vision to happen (Scruggs & Swerdlow, 1985).

John Champlain had a vision to radically reform the Johnson City, New York, schools in a period of ten years. When he became superintendent in 1978, the Johnson City schools were an educational disaster. Within five years, Champlain led the district to some amazing results. Employing the belief that all children can learn at high levels, and relying on Ben Bloom's mastery learning model, Champlain's reforms enabled his first graders to perform a full grade above their grade level, and his fifth graders to perform a grade and a half above their level. Students in the eighth grade performed nearly three years above their grade level—a feat believed to be impossible! Before 1979, only 10 percent of the graduates of Johnson City schools entered higher education, and 40 percent dropped out in the ninth grade to find jobs in the local shoe factory. John Champlain became a celebrity, with stories appearing in the *New York Times* and frequent appearances on TV talk shows. I visited the Johnson City schools in 1982 and found the test results and classroom successes to be valid. People from around the globe came to see this miracle that Champlain and his team had built.

How did John Champlain take this low-achieving system and turn it around? First, he took a risk during the job interview by telling the school board of his vision, which included the goal of higher standards and achievement if the board would support him when the change process began, causing some upheaval among the teaching and administrative staff. He warned them that he would need money to help carry out his vision. The board was so desperate for some successes that they hired Champlain and promised their support. During the first year, Champlain described his vision over and over to all who would listen in the hope of attracting a few devotees to his cause. A handful of teachers and administrators came aboard, and Champlain conducted the staff development activities himself and invited others to attend. His evangelistic zeal began to pay off during the second year when more teachers, mostly at the elementary level, began attending training sessions, and student test scores improved for the first time. Within four years, the excitement for change and being a part of a new era in the Johnson City schools caught on—with some exceptions at the high school. Champlain was able to breathe life into his vision in five short years.

A young principal from a poor West Virginia school was so impressed with what he had read about the Johnson City miracle that he loaded 21 of his teachers in a yellow school bus and drove them to Johnson City to learn the mastery teaching and learning model. In two years, the success among the students in his West Virginia school was so impressive that he was named state principal of the year. Again, we have one person, one vision, and amazing success.

VISIONS REQUIRE PATIENCE AND MONEY

The difficulty that leaders face in making visions happen is twofold. First, many administrators give up on their visions too soon. In a tight job market, most of us like to eat regularly and clothe our families. The overzealous approach by some administrators has produced joblessness. Joan of Arc died for her cause, but educational leaders need to prolong their stay and use good judgment about when to hold 'em and when to fold 'em. If a community gets into a feeding frenzy about the science of evolution versus creationism or intelligent design, whole language learning, self-esteem programs, or any other program that causes a major stir, the administrator has to decide whether to be Joan of Arc and attack or choose to use different language for the programs and live to fight another day.

A practical way to keep the vision alive in a time of right-wing and other anti–public school activity is to invite every citizen to contribute to the school visioning process. A word of advice—use the word "vision" with some caution because some people believe that visions appear only to the spiritualists or to those who are two pages shy of a book. One such school district that invites contributions is that of Lewisville, Texas. They seek input from the community on a regular basis by conducting a comprehensive needs assessment every five years and annual spot checks to test the community waters. In an effort to involve as wide a range of groups and individuals as possible, the board and administration decided on a comprehensive, communitywide school needs assessment with a variety of community meetings to invite people to tell the school officials what the patrons wanted the students in Lewisville to know in math, science, language arts, and social studies by the end of the fifth, eighth, and twelfth grades. A community survey was designed based on communitywide input and sent to a stratified random sample. Even though the survey instrument was pages long with detailed items, an astonishing 40 percent returned the surveys for analysis. The receptivity came from the careful planning by the board and administration to include the most vocal critics, senior citizens, students, parents, educators, and members of the business and professional communities. The findings of the questionnaire will lead to much greater acceptance by the community—especially the religious right and other vocal adversaries—and the change pill will be much easier for them to swallow when it comes.

Risk taking is much safer when the homework has been done and the direction of the wind is under constant surveillance. There are times in our administrative lives when a cause is worth losing a job for. However, it is good to remember what the old hunting guide said, "Never shoot over the horse's head until the horse is ready." School leaders must remember to learn the ins and outs of any community or organization before they jump up and shoot. The leader must possess patience, a high boiling point, and a burning vision to build new and exiting programs for students or clients. The pressures of leadership offer new challenges when demands for higher performance increase and limited resources are available. However, great leaders respond to difficult challenges while others seek the security of maintaining the status quo. The ingredients for effective change— patience while the community comes around, a high boiling point, and a burning vision to build a new and exciting program for students or clients—are an explosive mixture, but leadership is no challenge if the dangers or the excitement are missing in the journey.

Peter Senge, in his book *The Fifth Discipline* (1990), presents one model to help leaders cope with the vicissitudes of change. He reinforces the need for leaders to become systems-oriented in order to understand the forces surrounding change efforts. He believes that the core of any organization is its ability to bring people together to learn new ideas. His "learning organization" concept enables organizations to deal with significant systems problems and move successfully into the future. Senge believes that the learning organization is primarily designed to help people embrace change. People in learning organizations can look forward to creating, not merely reacting to, the new world as it emerges. It takes time to become an effective learning organization and for team members to develop the skill needed to help them change their work patterns and to interact with others in the organization. This model is the only feasible way to lead people to share a vision.

The content of a shared vision cannot be dictated from on high but must emerge from shared visions. The most powerful motivator is one's own personal vision. The learning organization prizes individual visions and aspirations and builds its future around them. Jack Welch, General Electric's former CEO, kept his learning organization alive through frequent meetings of all employees to create the future. His sessions stressed out-of-the-box thinking or, as he says, "boundaryless" sessions. No rules are established, and all ideas are considered. Perhaps that is why General Electric has grown so dramatically since Welch took over. Risk taking can be reduced if others are involved in the venture. A lone wolf is easy prey when the pack goes in another direction. It is prudent to be safe rather than sorry; remember, change is difficult for all of us unless we thought of the change first or we are involved from the very beginning. It is not a sign of weakness to revision when your initial vision loses its usefulness or falls on deaf ears. It is your decision about how far and how long you stray from the pack to seek your dream.

A second difficulty in transforming the vision into reality is the allocation of resources, especially money. If the foundation to the vision is to be built, the money must be there somewhere. If a school has created a collective vision through a democratic process that empowered teachers, students, staff, and parents, the prospects are better for locating external funding through state and federal school improvement assistance programs. Schools that are striving to build learning organizations where collaborative activity is prized and the entire community supports the instructional programs more easily find the resources for enrichment activities for the students. Unless school administrators and the teaching staff create a vision for the school that stresses student learning, team-building, and community involvement, funding agencies and corporations are reluctant to add their support. Without new leadership and a new vision for the school or school system, the local and state funding agencies will turn their attention to school leaders who will rally a community for quality and high standards. Funding proposals that stress collaboration, long-range planning, and clear benchmarks for student achievement are generally successful.

My colleagues, Linda Skrla and Jim Scheurich, shared this success story about making a vision happen. Steve Kinney, principal of Tice Elementary School in Galena Park, Texas, has a very clear vision about helping all students succeed. While Steve was provided limited funding for his project, he used the funds to directly impact the success of classroom teachers and the students. He says, "It's all about getting the *right kids* in the *right place* to get the help they need at the *right time.*" His vision inspired him and his teachers to keep close tabs on all students who needed special help with their test scores. All of the students identified as at risk of failing one or more of the sections of the state assessment were given personal attention each day. The students at Tice are 43 percent African American, 52 percent Latino, 4 percent Caucasian, 79 percent economically disadvantaged, and 24 percent English language learners.

By 2005, at least 98 percent of all students and all subgroups of students at Tice passed *all* sections of the state assessments, and the percentage of student groups earning "commended" performance acknowledgments was more than double the state average in many areas. Kinney made his vision happen by being a servant leader to his faculty and all 800 students and their families, creating a flexible, data-driven system, and communicating information clearly to the teachers in order to match individual students' learning needs with the appropriate instructional resources. Steve Kinney refused to quit on any of his kids, and they now have the skills and self-esteem to succeed in education and in life.

If leaders desire to transform their team visions into reality, then time and reflection are needed to facilitate careful planning and team-building. Team-building and the use of teams are overlooked areas. Peter Drucker, writing in *The Atlantic Monthly* in November 1994, emphasizes the importance of teams in the knowledge society by indicating that creative individuals in teams will work to improve organizations. New leadership is required to manage these talented, team-oriented organizations toward great productivity. Careful planning involving all stakeholders and continuing to focus on the welfare of the "generic kid" while keeping the overall system in focus will not solve the funding problem, but funding agencies and corporations are steering more grants to schools with a vision of success and empowerment of the entire learning community.

VISIONARIES ARE RISK TAKERS

Education and educators are frequently perceived as conservative non–risk takers who seek to maintain the status quo. Exceptions to the conservative security seekers are legion in education, but the perception is still prominent about school personnel. The story below is of one such individual, the risks he took, and the persistence he showed to achieve both personal and professional success.

Dr. Willis Mackey took a circuitous path to make his vision happen. Willis has been a risk taker since graduating from high school in Luling, Texas, where he was the state's number one running back prospect. Rather than attend a Texas university, Willis moved a long way from home and enrolled at the University of Washington. After a successful freshman year, Willis became homesick, quit the team, and returned closer to home—to the University of Oklahoma, where he sustained an injury that prevented playing football. After that disappointment he transferred to Southwest Texas State University (now Texas State University) to complete his degree. Even though he was proud of the degree, he felt unfulfilled because he had quit at the University of Washington. He moved to Newton, Texas, where he progressed from classroom teacher and football coach to high school principal and then to the position of superintendent. In spite of his rapid ascension to the top job, he still felt unsuccessful as a person. After some difficulties with school board members over building safety issues, Mackey met me and College Station, Texas, school superintendent Dr. Jim Scales to talk about his future. We advised him to apply for the superintendent position in Navasota, Texas, and apply for admission to the doctoral program at Texas A&M University. He got the job (he was Navasota's first African American superintendent) and he completed his doctorate two years later. At the same time he led the Navasota schools out of a history of low performance, especially among students of color and from poverty, to "recognized" status in Texas assessment rankings. In spite of these outstanding achievements, Willis still felt that he had to close the circle at the University of Washington. During the summer after receiving his doctorate, Willis flew his family to Seattle, entered the university's football stadium, and stood at the 50-yard line. He hugged his family, looked up in triumph, and declared himself a winner!

He closed the circle by completing his doctorate, turning around the lives of many children of color and poverty, and earning self-respect and the respect of others who admired his accomplishments. As a result of Dr. Mackey's outstanding leadership as superintendent at Navasota, he was selected to lead a much larger district in Port Arthur, Texas. Port Arthur recruited Mackey because they also endured low student achievement scores, excessive school dropouts, governance issues among certain board members and the community, and inadequate school funding. During his first challenging year laboring over critical school district problems, Hurricane Rita plowed through Port Arthur and left it in shambles. The city and the schools were severely damaged, and the schools were shut down for several weeks while emergency crews, the Red Cross, FEMA, and other rescue and repair efforts began. Mackey became a key leader in rallying support from city, state, and FEMA and other national groups to begin rebuilding the city and his school district. Later, after a presentation at Texas A&M University, Mackey was asked, "How did you pull others together to reopen the schools in a remarkably brief time?" Mackey the servant leader responded, "Because the kids needed to be back in school, I perhaps bent a few rules and perhaps overstepped my authority, but, someone had to step up. If people needed food, clothing, and fresh water, city officials and peace officers helped me get what the people needed, and we asked for permission later."

Risk takers may not always find success in all ventures, but Dr. Willis Mackey had a vision to serve others, communicated that vision to others, and had the courage to persist toward the vision. For the children and families he helped during some very difficult times, their superintendent was a winner.

CONCLUSIONS

Clear, shared visions have a magnetic pull if people are inspired and empowered to help make the visions happen. Individuals can feel alone with their visions unless leadership encourages the visions to be shared with colleagues. A vision that may be too abstract or silly to some may be concrete and serious to others. If the leader(s) can blend individual visions into a school or agency vision, then making the vision happen is possible and creates a symbol of hope for the organization. If the group feels the energy and creative tension in a vision, and the vision is a shared challenge, then the vision can come to pass. Individuals who have a passion for their visions and can persuade others to help make the vision happen are leaders. If a vision is to become a reality, careful planning, time for reflection, and adequate resources are imperative. Impatient managers who run with a vision too fast for those who must make the vision happen will never see a vision fulfilled. A delicate balance between the zeal to make changes and the patience to train and empower others is difficult to manage. The leadership balance and a team plan to seek necessary resources can help leaders become the visionaries they wish to be. Remember, to make visions happen, leaders must place the welfare of others first, serve those others, and then serve themselves. Dreams and visions by leaders can inspire others to extraordinary accomplishments. Leaders for the new millennium must have a dream and share it with others to make it come true.

CHAPTER FIVE

Staff Development Techniques to Envision and Create Real-World Programs

N ow that you are pumped to create a collective vision and watch the success of your effort pay off in high student or client satisfaction and an excitement for team learning and sharing, what gimmicks or techniques will you use and how will you engage others in the long, difficult journey? What thought process will you adopt to turn your staff into enthusiastic professionals who will give you the respect you deserve? Old Casey Stengel, the famous former New York Yankee manager, knew the value of great team play when he defined leadership as "gettin' paid for home runs somebody else hits" (Amundson, 1988, p. 7). Casey Stengel realized and other successful leaders realize that they must depend on specialists who can produce the goods. The late Peter Drucker (1993) believed that the new knowledge society was moving away from the generalist to the specialist, who must be team oriented. He encouraged managers to stress the importance of team workers rather than individuals to stay on the leading edge of the knowledge explosion.

The remainder of this chapter will present futuring strategies to help you and your staff become more visionary and better team players. Stephen Covey (1990) tells us to "begin with the end in mind" (p. 44). This should be used as a frame of reference or, as Covey refers to it, a personal mission statement. Because personal visions are the most motivating, people need this "inside-out" (p. 62) view to keep them on course. Having the end in view is not only motivating, it is also fun to share with others. Also, the degree to which each group member feels in control of his or her life and job role will determine the extent to which he or she will contribute to a collaborative effort. A leader who will share power and control and articulate a vision of a high-performing organization will help create the self-esteem and efficacy among staff to help make the vision come true. It is important, then, to invite staff to help plan their own staff development. The following ideas are good starting points for that important dialogue.

WORKSHOP ACTIVITY #1: USING THE GOODYEAR BLIMP TO CREATE A GROUP VISION

Introduce this activity by giving all workshop participants this assignment: "If you could rent the Goodyear blimp and fly it over your community or state in the year 2015, what three of your individual professional accomplishments would you like to be able to flash on the side of the blimp for all to see?" After these personal visions are written down by each individual, ask each of them to turn to the person to their right or left and share their visions of their accomplishments. This exercise breaks down barriers between people and gives a feeling of self-esteem and confidence in ideas that most of us do not usually talk about.

After all participants have shared their visions with a partner, divide participants into groups of 8 to 10 persons, keeping partners together, and ask each individual to share his or her partner's accomplishments with this small group. In each group, the person who had the most recent birthday can be the recorder of each accomplishment on a flip chart for the small group to see. Then ask the group to look for patterns in the accomplishments in 2015 and seek the group's ideas on what each individual can do to assist the members to accomplish their visions. In all likelihood, several themes will emerge from the desired accomplishments, and the genesis of a collective vision will become obvious. After the group vision takes some shape, rewrite it on the flip chart.

After a refreshment break, ask each small group to appoint a spokesperson to stand and describe to the entire workshop crowd the collective group vision and any individual visions that may diverge from the group vision. This step ensures individuality and respect for out-of-the-box thinking. Someone should be designated to collect all of the groups' flipcharts and prepare a collective set of staff visions for 2015. These visions can become a driving force in developing a district or system vision. I have used versions of this visioning process with cooperative extension professionals, law enforcement leaders, Phillip Morris executives, church members, school superintendents, principals, and teachers. It is especially effective in districtwide efforts to build a system vision and with site-based teams who need to alter or revision based on unforeseen factors that have changed over time.

WORKSHOP ACTIVITY #2:
THE HUNTSVILLE, TEXAS, MODEL: CREATING BELIEFS, CONVICTIONS, VISIONS, AND ACTIONS

The following ideas represent a combination of my own workshop strategies and those used by Peter Bishop and his colleagues at the Institute for Futures Research at the University of Houston–Clear Lake. The purpose of this second exercise is to create a vision and related belief statements for your school, business, or unit, to figure out how to share that vision, and to make that vision happen. This activity is highlighted with a step-by-step account of the visioning process that was used during 2005–2006 by the Huntsville, Texas, Independent School District to create a caring, high-performing school district by 2015. The activity is motivational to participants and it works. Announce to the group that it is now ten years from whatever today's date is, and that they (i.e., educators, agency leaders, government leaders, etc.—depends on the group) have been selection by a national or international organization as the most outstanding organization of its kind (i.e., school district, school, agency, city, company, etc.) in the United States. Break the large group into teams of six to eight persons, and instruct each team to think of three or four beliefs, convictions, visions, or actions that they created or took nine or ten years earlier that inspired the organization to earn this wonderful day of recognition. Ask a scribe from each team to write these beliefs, convictions, visions, and actions on a flip chart in preparation for sharing with the larger group.

Next, announce to everyone in the room that the president of the United States, the governor, and the U.S. secretaries of education and labor will soon arrive along with the global news network to interview each group about their phenomenal success since 2006. Then pretend to actually introduce the dignitaries, and ask a member of each team to share their three or four beliefs, convictions, visions, or actions created or taken nine or ten years earlier that led to this international recognition as the most child-centered (use the words *client-centered* if working with a noneducation group) and high-performing school, school district, university, agency, etc. This activity creates a lot of enthusiasm and laughter, since some presenters are better actors or clowns than others, and the ideas on the flip charts usually represent the best visionary thinking for writing a new vision or revising an old vision, belief, mission statement, or goals. Advise the organizational leaders to record all ideas and consider their use in the next strategic plan.

A complete example of this model follows. In September of 2005, I was invited to conduct an extensive strategic visioning process with the Huntsville, Texas, Independent School District. The superintendent, Dr. Richard Montgomery, with the help of his school board, staff, and others, appointed 90 citizens as members of the Huntsville Council for Excellence. These individuals included university administrators, city officials, ministers, middle and high school students, parents with or without students in school, medical doctors, business owners, educators, law enforcement leaders, criminal justice personnel, employees of the state prison system, and journalists. All council members received letters of invitation that included a detailed description of the planning process and that stressed each council member's involvement in creating a set of belief statements that the schools would rely on for the coming decade.

Stage 1

The first meeting was held in October in the Huntsville High School library, where the 90 council members were seated in groups of 10 around nine tables. After Dr. Montgomery welcomed the council and reinforced the reason each person was selected for this important process, he shared his vision, which centered on continuous improvement toward not merely exemplary schools, but schools of excellence. He expressed his thanks to the council members for giving their time and talent to help ensure that every current Huntsville student and those in the future would be provided with excellent schools. Dr. Montgomery urged the crowd to work with him, the entire staff, and the school board to create a set of beliefs that would drive their schools to seek excellence in every way. While the district had been successful over its long history, Dr. Montgomery went on to say, global challenges now called for a new and stronger resolve to strengthen the schools by creating a more rigorous and relevant curriculum, adopting new teaching strategies, and finding better uses of technology to prepare Huntsville graduates for a more competitive job market and the global community.

He then introduced me to the council, and, using an accompanying slide presentation, I described a series of current and future challenges that face all high school students, and I stressed the importance of total community support in assuring that all students would be prepared to face increasing global competition, especially from China and India. Drawing on the work of Thomas Friedman, author of *The World Is Flat* (2005), and his "ten forces that flattened the world," we discussed why stronger skills in math, science, communications, and technology were critical for every Huntsville student. I then put up a slide with the African proverb found on page 114 in Friedman's book:

Every morning in Africa, a gazelle wakes up.

It knows it must run faster than the fastest lion or it will be killed.

Every morning a lion wakes up.

It knows it must outrun the slowest gazelle or it will starve to death.

It doesn't matter whether you are a lion or a gazelle.

When the sun comes up, you better start running.

Friedman writes (and I read), "I don't know who is the lion and who is the gazelle, but I do know this: Ever since the Chinese joined the WTO (World Trade Organization), both they and the rest of the world have had to run faster and faster" (p. 114).

Stage 1 ended with comments about the power of visioning to create the future and about how strong core beliefs and values will promote districtwide support for improvements in the Huntsville schools.

Stage 2

I told the 90 council members, "Let's now jump into the future to 2015 and read the headlines in the *Huntsville Item* newspaper and on the Internet." My next slide read,

HUNTSVILLE ISD, THE NATION'S BEST

The Huntsville ISD received word today, October 11, 2015, that the White House, The U.S. Chamber of Commerce, and the Baldridge Foundation have selected the Huntsville Independent School District as the most student-centered and high-performing district in the United States.

Next I informed the groups that each one included a facilitator who was a district teacher or administrator who had been trained earlier in the evening to lead them through the Cooperative Process and that each group needed to select a recorder by determining among themselves who had the smallest pet. After each group selected its recorder, I said,

Within the hour, the president of the United States, two executives with the Baldridge Foundation, the president of the National Chamber of Commerce, the U.S. secretary of education, and the mayor and members of the city council will arrive. They will ask each of your groups to respond to the following question: 'Back on October 11, 2005, what three or four beliefs, convictions, visions, or actions did you record that guided your district to this day of celebration and national recognition?' Be prepared to share these three or four beliefs, convictions, visions, or actions with these visiting dignitaries and the Global News Network. How will you explain how those three or four beliefs, convictions, or visions or actions led to becoming the nation's best school district on October 11, 2015?

Each group was provided with a big writing pad, a felt marking pen, and writing pads and pencils for each member. (Snacks were also well received.)

The group facilitators then read the charge to each group member and explained the Cooperative Process. This process is a modification of the Nominal Group Process made popular by Delbecq, Van DeVen, and Gustafson in the mid-1970s and modified for educational staff development activities by Jim Sweeney and others (see Cunningham, 1982). The cooperative process consists of five rounds to help groups solve current problems or develop visionary ideas for creating the future.

Silent Generation Round. The facilitator repeats the question and asks each member to write down three or four beliefs, convictions, visions, or actions that were recorded or taken beginning in 2005 that led to this great day for the district. This should take approximately five minutes.

Recording Round. As soon as all group members have completed their lists, the facilitator says, "Now, we will go clockwise around the table and have each member give one idea (i.e., belief, conviction, vision, or action) at a time to be recorded on the big flip chart pad." The facilitator encourages the members to keep their ideas brief to assist the recorder, who is attempting to write with the felt pen on the big pad. The facilitator continues around the circle, asking each member in turn for another thought. Members can pass on any round and contribute later when ideas come to them. When all ideas are recorded and displayed (usually this takes two or more big sheets of paper), the recorder numbers them.

Clarification Round. As soon as all items are numbered, the facilitator instructs the group to clarify the meaning or intent of all items. This is the best time to combine selected items if those providing the ideas agree.

Clear Out Round. The facilitator now says, "Since we have more items than we need, let's see if we can reduce the list to the nine or ten we feel most strongly about. This will be by vote rather than consensus, but to reach consensus may take all day on some of these ideas. Now, place your elbows on the table with your palms up and your fists closed. When I call out item number one, if you wish for it to remain on the list, open your fist. If you want to eliminate the item keep your fist closed. Majority rules, but discussion can still go on to clarify each item's meaning until the final vote." After the vote, the recorder renumbers the items to prepare for the final voting.

Final Vote Round. The facilitator asks group members to keep their elbows on the table and prepare to use fingers to vote on the three or four best beliefs, convictions, visions, or actions that led to this great day in 2016. He or she informs the group that all five fingers can be used for only one item: "You may use four, three, two, one, or zero as many times as you wish, but five only once. Now when I read each item number, show a number of fingers that represents how important you believe that item is, and the recorder and I will count the number of fingers and the recorder will write the total number of votes by each item." After the final vote on all items, the recorder adds up the total number of votes for each item. The three or four with the highest vote totals are considered the best beliefs, convictions, visions, or actions; these will be orally presented to the visiting dignitaries.

Stage 3

Next, in a raised voice, I said to the 90 council members that "the president and the other dignitaries have arrived at the door" and announced, "Ladies and gentlemen, the president of the United States!" I asked them to rise and we had a laugh and time to stretch. I then went from group to group with a handheld mike—if there is no real mike a pen or pencil works—and asked the facilitator to tell the president and the world watching on television what three or four beliefs, convictions, visions, or actions they created or took back in October 2005 that led to national recognition as the nation's best school district in 2015. After each group reported, I showered them with praise and moved to the next group.

Stage 4

The flip chart pads were collected and each item was recorded and prepared for distribution at the next council meeting. Over 100 ideas were recorded in the recording round; these were narrowed down to approximately 40 items in the final vote round.

Stage 5

The final 40 beliefs, convictions, visions, and actions were mailed to the 90 members of the superintendent's council for excellence before the next meeting in November 2005. During this meeting, each of the ten groups was instructed to review the 40 items and attempt to place the items into specific categories. The three categories were *Knowledge, Skills, and Attitudes for Academic Excellence; Knowledge, Skills, and Attitudes for Career Excellence;* and *Knowledge, Skills, and Attitudes for Character Excellence.* This activity proved successful and the reordered items were prepared for the next meeting in December, which was to be attended by nine representatives—one selected by each group.

Stage 6

The nine group representatives were mailed copies of the 40 beliefs, convictions, visions, and actions as they had been sorted into the three areas of excellence—academic, career, and character. I asked the ten leaders to collaborate on creating statements from the forty items that would become the driving statements to steer the district to become the nation's best in 2015. I stressed the need to create statements that would be recommended to the board of education by the superintendent for adoption by the board. We discussed the need to have statements that represented the quest for excellence in each of the three areas. Thus, we began the hard work with the words, "We believe that. . . ."

In three hours the creative, hardworking team of nine produced seven core belief statements that were distributed to the other 81 members of the council for their consideration.

Stage 7

On December 12, 2005, the council of 90 met and the belief statements developed by their team leaders were discussed and revised to include some rewording and changing of the order. The superintendent's staff e-mailed the revised version to all council members for their approval. At a meeting on January 17, 2006, the council reviewed the belief statements once more, and it also reviewed existing vision and mission statements and district goals to determine if they aligned with the council's belief statements.

The final meeting was conducted on February 7 with 10 representatives; this group included three members of minority groups,

Huntsville Independent School District

CORE BELIEFS AND VISION

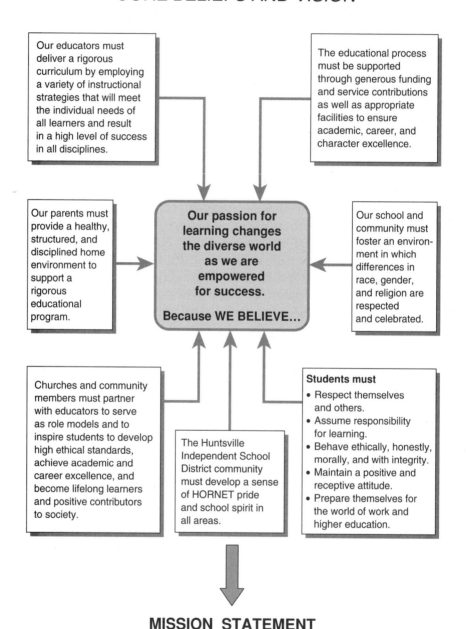

Our educators must deliver a rigorous curriculum by employing a variety of instructional strategies that will meet the individual needs of all learners and result in a high level of success in all disciplines.

The educational process must be supported through generous funding and service contributions as well as appropriate facilities to ensure academic, career, and character excellence.

Our parents must provide a healthy, structured, and disciplined home environment to support a rigorous educational program.

Our passion for learning changes the diverse world as we are empowered for success.

Because WE BELIEVE...

Our school and community must foster an environment in which differences in race, gender, and religion are respected and celebrated.

Churches and community members must partner with educators to serve as role models and to inspire students to develop high ethical standards, achieve academic and career excellence, and become lifelong learners and positive contributors to society.

The Huntsville Independent School District community must develop a sense of HORNET pride and school spirit in all areas.

Students must
- Respect themselves and others.
- Assume responsibility for learning.
- Behave ethically, honestly, morally, and with integrity.
- Maintain a positive and receptive attitude.
- Prepare themselves for the world of work and higher education.

MISSION STATEMENT

> The Huntsville Independent School District will establish a family atmosphere with students, parents, and the community to provide comprehensive, equitable, educational experiences based on national and state curriculum and testing standards and providing innovative teaching in a caring, safe environment. Student progress and personal development will be monitored and measured to ensure that each student advances to his or her highest potential. The educators, parents, community members, churches, and other agencies will provide the support for a comprehensive, rigorous curriculum and other student development programs and facilities to ensure the overall development of each student. Each student will experience the latest learning technologies in advanced math, science, communication skills, and appreciation of the arts in order to become a competitive player in a diverse, global environment.

two high school students, and three others from the business community. With input from Dr. Montgomery, the group revisited the seven core belief statements, and, after considerable discussion, they created a brief, compelling vision statement to drive the belief statements. Next, a mission statement was written as an action guide for the vision and belief statements. The group then selected the two high school students to make the presentation to the school board on February 16. The group of 10 decided that t-shirts would be made for the two students and Dr. Montgomery for the board presentation. The t-shirts read "Hornet Pride" on the front and "Vision Statement" on the back. In addition, all of the flip chart sheets—including every idea from the first meeting to the last—were placed on the wall in the board room.

The vision, belief, and mission statements were presented by the students to the board of education with supporting comments from council members. After board approval, the statements became policy and the benchmark beliefs and foundation for all decisions that will be made by the board and the school administration for the next few years. The vision is to keep a clear and determined focus on these statements to drive the district to the honor that will be bestowed by the president and the others on October 11, 2015.

WORKSHOP ACTIVITY #3: SCHOOLS FOR THE FUTURE

This exercise helps a faculty envision a school that provides total human services for all students; that is, the school provides health care, family services, etc., in addition to academics.

Stage 1

Start by dividing staff into groups with five or six members; each group should include faculty that teach different grades and different subject areas. Give each group a flip chart pad on an easel and felt tip pens. After each group selects a group facilitator by determining which member received the most worthless Christmas gift, have them begin by listing the kinds of skills, attributes, knowledge, and values that the faculty would like the students to have when students graduate from their school district. After listing these on flip charts and clarifying for duplication of ideas, ask the group to list the learning environments and teaching activities that are most conducive to learning these desired skills, attitudes, knowledge, and values. This second step is to help the teaching staff focus on educating the whole child and to look beyond the daily pressures and restraints of state-developed high-stakes exams and No Child Left Behind (NCLB) mandates (Montgomery, 1997). Participants may wish to refer to the resources in the list at the end of this section for ideas. Total time for this activity is 2 ½ hours.

Stage 2

The next task is for the members of each group to render a drawing of their school on the flip chart pad. The drawing will include the shape and size of the facility, the learning areas, and external features (i.e., recreation areas, community agency space, etc.). Total time for this activity is 2 hours.

Resources for Workshop Activity #3

Futuring: The Exploration of the Future, by Ed Cornish, offers a wide variety of contextual ideas that impact school and university planning in an age of distance and Web-based education (Bethesda, MD: World Future Society, 2004).

Selected articles from *The Futurist* will be useful; this journal is published six times annually by the World Future Society, 4916 St. Elmo Ave., Bethesda, MD 20814.

Schools That Learn, by Peter Senge et al., is a wonderful resource for creating learning communities for the future (New York: Doubleday, 2000).

School Empowerment, edited by M. Richardson, M. Flanagan, and K. Lane, includes a chapter titled "A Vision of the Future and the New School Principal," by J. Hoyle (Lancaster, PA: Technomic, 1995).

WORKSHOP ACTIVITY #4: FUTURE SOCIETY PROPOSITIONS

This activity prepares participants to develop future scenarios by challenging them to look at numerous propositions about the future (Bartos & Hanson, 1976; Rogers, 1985). Each person will respond to a questionnaire; this process requires approximately 10 minutes.

The questionnaire is composed of propositions about our future society in the decade 2006–2016. These propositions are the result of intensive review of the futuristic literature. Two opinions are asked of participants: their opinion of the likelihood that these events will come to pass sometime between 2006 and 2016, and their opinion of the impact these events will have on their fields (e.g., education, business, law enforcement) if they come to pass. Participants should thus use two scales to score each statement:

Likelihood of Occurrence	Impact on Your Field
1 = low (0–20 percent chance)	1 = low (0–20 percent chance)
2 = moderately low (21–40 percent chance)	2 = moderately low (21–40 percent chance)
3 = average (41–60 percent chance)	3 = medium (41–60 percent chance)
4 = moderately high (61–80 percent chance)	4 = moderately high (61–80 percent chance)
5 = high (81–100 percent chance)	5 = high (81–100 percent chance)

For example, for the time scale, if participants believe an event will have occurred by 2015, they would rate the item a 4 or 5. If they believe that an event will not occur in this time frame, they would rate the item a 1 or 2. For the impact scale, the question is, "If this event occurs, what impact will it have or your field?" If a significant impact would occur, participants should enter a 4 or 5. If little or no impact would result, they should enter a 1 or 2.

Optional: Where participants rate a proposition as high in impact on their fields (score 4 or 5), have them jot down a word or phrase to suggest what will be affected.

After the class or group has completed the inventory, place individuals into groups of four to six and ask them to discuss and defend their responses.

Likelihood of Occurrence		Impact on Your Field
	1. Little progress will be made toward world peace.	
	2. The greenhouse effect will cause the polar ice caps to melt and cause worldwide floods.	
	3. The Internet will become available to all people on earth.	
	4. Distance education will replace traditional classrooms.	
	5. Life expectancy will expand to an average of 80 years in the United States.	
	6. The U.S. government will demand public access to financial records of all citizens.	
	7. Hydrogen will replace fossil fuels for automobiles, buses, and trucks.	
	8. Marriage will lose its importance among younger generations.	
	9. No-fault divorce will become the norm in all states.	
	10. The labor force will be replaced by robots.	

Likelihood of Occurrence		Impact on Your Field
	11. Food and fiber production will become fully automated and the family farm will be eliminated.	
	12. Corporations will give greater weight to employees' personal concerns in making personnel decisions.	
	13. Protection of the global environment will become a national goal.	
	14. Research in the social sciences will produce powerful new tools that will be used in both the public and private sectors to enhance consensus decision making.	
	15. Researchers in education and business administration will find direct links between university preparation and successful practices of schools principals, superintendents, business managers, and agency administrators.	
	16. Medical science will perfect stem cell research that cures cancer, replaces organs, and prevents prenatal health problems for children and mothers.	
	17. Donor banks will increase capacity so transplant organs will be available for all who desire them.	
	18. Abortion will no longer be a major issue.	
	19. People will continue to refuse to buy irradiated food products.	
	20. Megachurches will become a relic of the past in favor of smaller home churches.	
	21. The world population will grow to 12 billion.	
	22. Immigration will pump the U.S. population up to 350 million.	
	23. The percentage of women school superintendents and corporate CEOs will increase to over 20 percent.	

(Continued)

(Continued)

Likelihood of Occurrence		Impact on Your Field
	24. There will be increased governmental control of the national economy.	
	25. India and China will replace the United States as world economic powers.	
	26. War with China will cause global disaster.	
	27. There will be a wider variety of family styles in addition to the traditional husband-wife-children family unit.	
	28. Health care will be readily available to all U.S. citizens.	

WORKSHOP ACTIVITY #5: SCENARIO WRITING AND APPLICATIONS

Scenario writing was made popular by the late Herman Kahn, author of books such as *On Thermonuclear War* (1960), *The Coming Boom* (1982), and *The Next 200 Years* (1986). Kahn directed the Hudson Institute and was a leading advisor and consultant for the White House, the Department of Defense, and major corporations. His most effective futures methodology was the scenario. He would study historical and current trends, global economics, politics, and new technologies before embarking on preparing three scenarios based on assumptions and three sets of data. This approach would offer Kahn's clients alternative futures (i.e., preferred, acceptable, unacceptable). He believed that we can choose which alternative we prefer and can have some influence on which alternative happens.

About Writing Scenarios

A scenario is developed by studying all possible information about a problem and projecting a broad range of trends, their likelihood of occurrence, and the degree of impact on the organization under study if the trends did occur. In writing scenarios, imagine your life at some future time—such as 10, 15, or 20 years from now. This process is known as *backcasting* from a position in the future to personal struggles, successes, earlier world events, etc. that influenced your imagined success. The scenario in Chapter 1 written by the high school junior is an example of leaping into the future and describing your job role, the world around you, your family, transportation systems, education systems and learning technologies, community development, and so on. Scenarios include descriptions of how you feel about your new world and what you have accomplished. They include the education and professional development that helped promote you to your exalted position in, say, 2015.

Scenario writing should follow immediately after earlier exercises that stressed imaging and futuring. The length of a scenario can range from one paragraph to several pages. The length for the following exercise is recommended to be no more than one page. This length will allow time for participants to share their masterpieces with each other. This sharing is fun and exciting and encourages creative out-of-the-box thinking. Scenarios contain the following benefits:

- They make us aware of potential pitfalls that may occur if a certain action is taken. Scenarios make it possible to consider the possible circumstances of a proposed action and assist us in altering the action to avoid negative consequences (Bishop, 1994).
- Scenarios give us an opportunity to think about our future successes as individuals and as organizations.
- All age groups, especially students, enjoy writing scenarios because they are not typical term research papers or reports. Elementary school teachers already know this. I have read scenarios by fourth graders that are research-based, creative, and well organized.
- Scenarios can rally others to work in teams to analyze alternative plans and actively participate in building programs.
- Scenarios spark imagination, create emotion, and bring about an awareness of broad trends and issues; scenarios are easy to read and they enable the individual to see how he or she fits into the scheme of things. Remember, personal visions are the most powerful.

Scenario Exercise

A suggested follow-up after workshop activities #3 and #4 is to ask participants to write a one-page personal scenario about their own successful future. Ask them to place themselves into a position of success in the years 2016–2020 and describe the world around them and what education and career steps they took to help them on life's journey of success. Allow 10 to 15 minutes for writing; then follow up as a roving reporter, and invite volunteers to share their futures with the entire group.

Effectiveness of Scenario Writing

In a recent workshop for young political hopefuls in Austin, Texas, I found an enthusiastic young African American woman who read about her future as governor in 20 years. Scenarios have a strong future pull about them, so who am I to question her election? Asking people to share their future creates good humor and deep reflection on preferred futures for all participants. Last year, a graduate student named Debbie, a talented musician, described her scenario to the class while playing a piano. She said, "I will own and manage my own school, which will stress music therapy, and will meet the love of my life named David." Recently, I ran into Debbie at the mall, and she ran up, hugged me, and exclaimed, "You are not going to believe this, but I recently got a job as a music therapist and I am engaged to be married in June. His name is David!" A coincidence? No one can predict the future, but scenarios can lead one's thinking in interesting directions.

Organizations, including schools, universities, cooperative extension programs, and other human service agencies, can move beyond the ordinary strategic planning processes that are often boring and viewed by the staff as something done by a consultant or committee. Staff interest in team planning can be raised to new, higher levels by conducting the exercises in this chapter and culminating with a series of scenarios to be examined by all stakeholders for possible action. In my 48 years in education, scenario writing is the most effective method I have found to motivate students of all ages and professionals to think seriously about their future and how the world will affect that future.

WORKSHOP ACTIVITY #6: THE DELPHI TECHNIQUE

The Oracle of Delphi, Greece, dating back to 1400 BC, held mystical powers of vision to advise kings about war, marriage, and fortunes.

The oracle relied on the directions and colors of smoke from burning animal entrails and other rituals for her predictions. Regardless of this dubious beginning, the Delphi technique has become a respected futures method. The Delphi technique is applied to seek expert opinion about what the future portends. This technique has become one of the most popular methods of forecasting future programs, problems, and events. It is a method to systematically gather information from independent experts on specific topics of interests. (This activity differs from those described previously because it is set up as an e-mail exchange rather than as a series of interactions for groups within a workshop. Conceivably it could also be used within a workshop; however, the e-mail approach described here provides a unique advantage, as described below.)

For example, one study was conducted by selecting 15 athletic directors in Division I universities and asking their opinions about the impact of Title IX on adequate funding for all athletic programs. Since the technique in this form eliminates face-to-face interactions of the panelists, they are free to respond without the influence of others that can be experienced in the cooperative process model. The technique involves several rounds of questions for the 10 to 15 expert panelists; they respond to the question or problem via e-mail or snail mail. The rounds of questions might include the following:

Round 1. The researcher asks the athletic directors to write five or six solutions to the financial problems created by Title IX.

Round 2. This round usually consists of a questionnaire developed from Round 1 with items requiring panelists' responses on an intensity scale of Always to Never or Strongly Agree to Strongly Disagree, with a 5- or 7-point range.

Round 3. For this round, researchers calculate the mean, median, and mode of the combined responses on the questionnaire. The results are sent to the panel, revealing the interquartile range of scores (the difference between the 25th and 75th percentiles), and showing how many of the panel's responses fall outside of this range.

According to Cunningham (1982), consensus is assumed to be achieved when a certain percentage of votes, a consensus percent, falls within the interquartile range. A cutoff percentage of 70 percent to 90 percent is typically used to determine if consensus is reached.

Normally, if the panelists' responses fall within the same quartile, there is little need to go for the next round. However, this rarely occurs on a controversial topic like Title IX.

Round 4. The next step is to return the statistical results to the panel and ask them to reconsider the others' responses and respond to the questionnaire again. If any of the panelists chooses to remain outside the range of the others, he or she is asked to provide a minority opinion in paragraph form.

Round 5. This paragraph is then sent to the other panelists for their thoughtful deliberations. This may or may not convince others to change their responses.

Round 6. The final round includes recalculating the interquartile range, plotting the location of each panelist's response in the distribution, and including individual written positions or opinions on the subject.

For instance, the athletic directors may conclude that some men's sports must be eliminated to support more women's teams. Or they may conclude that each sport must improve participation numbers to increase revenue for their own support.

For more in-depth information on the Delphi technique, see Chapter 8 in Cunningham's 1982 work, *Systematic Planning for Educational Change.* Also see Drain's 1998 dissertation, *Reform Trends Facing Athletic Programs in the 21st Century as Identified by Division I Athletics Directors.*

WORKSHOP ACTIVITY #7:
USING A SCENARIO TO INSPIRE VISIONING

The following scenario is part of a keynote address that I delivered to a meeting of members of the Gulf Coast Tech Prep Consortium. This vision of tech prep and its future possibilities is an example of how a scenario can be an excellent motivational device to focus a group on their own vision. I introduced the scenario by asking the audience to imagine reading an article from the *Houston Chronicle* on February 10, 2020:

Tech prep programs were given high praise by the keynote speaker at the twenty-second annual Gulf Coast Consortium Tech Prep Conference held in Houston yesterday. Dr. David Sanders, president of Power Infotech Systems, said, "I am impressed. This tech prep program serves over three million people in the Gulf Coast area and integrates the resources of public schools, higher education, government, business, and social service agencies into serving the needs of people. Education is really working." The conference was held in the new Tech Prep Center, which is a futuristic masterpiece. The center houses specialists in information technologies, urban planners, education and health specialists, and business and family counselors. These specialists facilitate the learning and development of students, teachers, and community members, enabling them to develop new job skills and self-esteem.

Equipped with the big four information technologies—computer networks, imaging technology, massive data storage, and artificial intelligence—the center and its staff are helping Gulf Coast citizens learn to use them more skillfully and effectively. Dr. Sanders told the audience that national information highways allow tech prep students and clients to communicate with anyone, anywhere, anytime. Through imaging technologies, students from preschool through graduate school can actually learn by doing. New job skills are mastered through virtual reality and other visual models. Equipped with color video phones connected to schools, homes, businesses, and learning centers, clients can send and receive digital visual information to and from classrooms, corporate boardrooms, businesses, and homes. Throughout the Gulf Coast region, students can beam up the Tech Prep Center and get help with math, languages, sciences, job skills, and personal counseling on financial or psychological problems. These interactive learning technologies have been a prime factor in the high achievement of students in the K-12 and community college systems. In addition, all Gulf Coast middle school, high school, and community college students are within 25 minutes of the Tech Prep Center via maglev high-speed rail. At the center, students can access classes at community colleges, high schools, universities, and corporations via interactive compressed video.

This remarkable development had its genesis in the 1980s and grew dramatically in the 1990s. In 2005, at the first annual Gulf Coast Conference, several visionaries gathered to create a successful future for tech prep. These leaders knew that the old image of vocational education was a barrier to the new image of tech prep. The old vocational programs, which were losing enrollment, were considered by some as not very demanding, and Carl Perkins funding for the faltering programs was in jeopardy. Through a process of revisioning a new tech prep model of success, a dream was begun. Integrating academic, career, and technology content with staff development to train teacher and workforce groups, a new integrated curriculum was initiated. This new contextual model changed the perception of career and technology education into meaning-centered education. Students were exposed to future career opportunities and experienced the reasons that math, English, languages, and science are critical to success in the labor force. Through mediated learning technologies, job site visits, and mentors, students and teachers at all levels viewed career and academic learning as one program. It was education with meaning and quality.

The quality of the Gulf Coast workforce is now considered the best in the South and Southwest. Dr. Sanders also stated that "the Gulf Coast area is among the top five most productive urban centers in America. We have two percent unemployment and fourth-highest per capita income, and violence and crime rates have been reduced over 70 percent since 2005." Many reasons are given for this phenomenal reversal, but observers pointed to the tech prep program leaders, who persuaded traditional educators and business and government leaders that every child, college bound or not, needs self-esteem and meaning. Tech prep educators knew that the jobs of the future were in the medical, business, engineering, and legal services; careers in air transportation and information, recreation, and health were also among those with bright futures. From 1989 to 1994, Texas led the nation in job growth and had the highest percentage of young people for the future workforce. This diverse multilingual future workforce needed skills and self-esteem to become productive members of society who could have a quality life in safe and caring communities. Education and job skills were the answer to a successful twenty-first century in the Gulf Coast area.

Back in the winter of 2005, the future was cloudy and frightening for those gathered at that first Tech Prep Conference. Regular public education programs were educating about 40 percent of the students. The others were sent into an information-based job market with minimum skills and little promise of success in life. Added to this was the high poverty rate, especially among minority youth from single-parent homes in the Gulf Coast region, and there existed a pattern of violence, fear, and day-to-day survival that was thrown to the schools to handle. The American dream for many of our kids in 2005 had become a nightmare of despair.

The education models in 2005 were not working, and tech prep leaders heeded the words of Margaret J. Wheatley, author of a 1992 book titled *Leadership and the New Science,* who believed that we create reality as we go along, not because we are not good planners, but because reality is difficult to find and the search can bring meaning to our lives and work.

With a vision for collaboration and a growing comfort with uncertainty, Gulf Coast Tech Prep Consortium members moved beyond the dream. These ideas might have languished, but fortunately, new Carl Perkins funds, state appropriations, client fees, and corporate and local funding made the dream a reality. The Tech Prep Center was completed six years ago, in 2014. Only a small number of those attending that first conference in February of 2005 believed that the facility would become a reality and that tech prep would dramatically give direction to education and the Gulf Coast area. The dream came true.

CONCLUSIONS

To become the leader who can persuade your staff to engage in futuring, you need to practice your futuring skills. Engage the staff and encourage them to improve their knowledge and skills and build a higher-performing team. As Mother Goose said, "Good, better, best; never rest until good is better and better best." Practice your skills of persuasion and visioning on a daily basis. Begin with a small steering committee and train them to train others in futuring using the exercises in this chapter, or arrange for yourself and the committee to attend futuring sessions offered by individuals or professional associations. Futuring encompasses the major components of other development activities, such as total quality management, quality circles, strategic planning, and team-building processes. Futuring conveys images of the future, captures the assumptions and forces affecting the future, and creates an excitement for team play. Max De Pree (1989), author of *Leadership Is an Art,* said it all about the importance of a leader keeping the ax of leadership sharp when he wrote, "In the end, it is important to remember that we cannot become what we need to be by remaining what we are" (p. 100). I hope that the exercises in this chapter will continue to sharpen the leadership and visioning saws that will not only enhance your career advancement, but also inspire those you lead to reach their highest life goals.

CHAPTER SIX

The Visionary Leader You Can Become

E nglish statesman and author Benjamin Disraeli said, "The secret of success is constancy of purpose." The greatest leaders believe in their purpose and perfect their craft. Pat Riley (1993), philosopher, former coach of the New York Knicks, and now coach of the Miami Heat, knows the dangers of resting on last year's performance and warns us by saying, "Excellence is the gradual result of always wanting to do better." This book is about how individuals can get better as visionary leaders for schools and other organizations.

All school administrators and educators, law enforcement leaders, and business executives I know want to get better at what they do. However, those I know who are constantly talking about the future are the ones who seem to get more done and with more flair. These individuals spend their time learning new ideas by talking to others and participating in workshops about change and how to bring it about. They realize that skills in futuring and visioning are critical to their success and to how they feel about themselves as leaders. Max De Pree (1989) understood this when he said, "The only kind of leadership worth following is based on vision" (p. 133). Many leading school superintendents said they like to think about the future and build a vision of what is best for kids, but they do not like to wait too long to make a decision. If they do, the school board and the staff think the superintendent is indecisive or burned out. School leaders tend to get bored without challenges and would prefer to be viewed as mover and shakers rather than visionaries and dreamers. Most visionaries are impatient about the status quo because their visions haunt them. Thus they face a dilemma: Should they build visions and bring others along to create ownership? Or should they address the impatience to make things happen *now?*

Social scientists have few clues about the makeup of charismatic visionary leaders. Jay Conger, in his book *The Charismatic Leader* (1989), presents his view of the characteristics of charismatic visionaries. He writes,

> Charismatic leaders were great information collectors with a difference—they used multiple and often apparently unrelated sources of information. . . . The second element of vision involves risk. Launching a new product or service . . . sometimes involves extreme risk. . . . Timing and serendipity are also critical elements in whether the strategic vision will ultimately materialize into success. (pp. 66, 67)

Conger and others have found that subordinates of visionaries tend to like their jobs more, work longer hours without complaint, trust colleagues and their leaders more, and have higher performance ratings than the followers of nonvisionary leaders (Conger, 1989). Visionary leaders seem to develop team loyalty around ideas and shared values. Also, visionaries can be iconoclasts by going against the grain, but they can also inspire staff to cultivate the organizational culture by using metaphors, shared symbols, mottos, and a sense of history and purpose to motivate others to rally to a cause.

The seven leaders I described in Chapter 2 were blessed with charisma and vision. The leaders I knew and those I didn't had that undefined ability to move ordinary people to extraordinary accomplishments. That is why I remember them and why history recorded them. They had a capacity for caring for others, clear communication, and a commitment to persist. These characteristics, then, are the legs on which to stand if you wish to improve your vision and be seen as a more charismatic leader.

LEADERS HAVE A SERVICE VISION

According to scholar Leonard Berry (1995) service vision is the reason some organizations reach the Fortune 500 level while others fail. These organizations are so service-centered that nothing is too good for the customer. In organizations with a service vision, clients are treated with respect, provided information when needed, and assured of immediate follow-up on the performance of the product or service. The capacity to care deeply is embedded in one's moral center and core values. How you acquire it is generally known in social science research. Childhood and all of its influences are considered the foundation for becoming a caring visionary leader.

Psychologist David McClelland (1978) has spent a career investigating the characteristics of high achievers. He has found that high achievers tend to have four basic behavioral characteristics: (1) the willingness to take moderate, calculated risks; (2) a preference for activities that provide rapid and precise information on the nature of problems as well as on performance; (3) intrinsic satisfaction in getting a job done well rather than dependence on extrinsic rewards; and (4) a preoccupation with completing a task, often at the expense of interpersonal relationships. Thus, a high need to achieve can get in the way of getting along and caring about others in the organization. The visionary leader for the future must be impatient to make visions happen, but only to the extent that others in the organization know that the leader is sensitive to their needs and will take the time to inform and train them for the challenge ahead. A visionary is not very valuable unless he or she can bring others along to help build the vision.

Caring for others is the motivator for most of us who chose education as a career and for others who have entered the ministry, youth work, or social welfare agencies. Albert Schweitzer gave up a prominent and lucrative medical practice to spend his life healing the sick in the jungles of Africa. Mother Teresa, a symbol of love for those destitute in India, could have chosen a less demanding and more comfortable life. Those of us who chose to educate others may not spend our lives among the sick and helpless, but our challenge to become servant leaders is equally important. Each time we explain our vision and attempt to persuade others to help us blaze a new path, we are asking them to believe in us and to go along with the risks of the unknown.

Futurist Joel Barker knows the value and the risks in developing a collective vision in any organization. The leader is ultimately responsible for the final product. It is the leader's vision, belief, and trust in others that can make a vision happen. Barker, in his video titled *The Power of Vision* (1991), says, "Vision without action goes nowhere; vision with action can change the world." Compassion for the well-being of others can produce the necessary action to make a dream become a reality.

Camille Lavington, an international image and marketing consultant, believes that when we serve others selflessly and help them achieve their highest goals, everyone will benefit from their abilities and achievements. Visionary leaders must have a cause beyond a personal agenda or self-enhancement.

People will follow servant leaders who model the team concept. Arlene Blum led nine other women to accomplish something that no other group of women had done. She led the American Women's Himalayan Expedition to reach the summit of Annapurna I, the tenth highest mountain in the world. She spoke the words of a true servant leader when she said of their accomplishment,

> We had to believe in ourselves enough to make the attempt in spite of social convention and two hundred years of climbing history in which women had been told that they didn't have the leadership experience and emotional stability necessary to climb the highest mountains. (Kouzes & Posner, 1987, p. 82)

Blum, a servant leader, persuaded and helped train nine other women to take a major risk. She told them of her vision and helped the other women gain the necessary skills and confidence to accept the challenge, and the mountain became theirs.

What, then, can you do to become a more caring person and leader? Because school reform has begun to change the face of education, a new, more caring leader is required to facilitate the changes. With greater emphasis on empowering others and fostering greater creativity and risk taking, principals and teachers must share the leadership functions. This systemic change to more bottom-up leadership is frequently viewed as a challenge to the power and autonomy of school boards and central office administrators and can create roadblocks to visions for faculty, students, and parents. However, the caring superintendent will shift the focus of power and authority to others to encourage the visioning process to flourish. Remember; when you become obsessed with your own importance, visions grow dim and the ability to motivate others dies. Unless the leader is viewed as a caring, serving person, others try to avoid him or her.

Robert K. Greenleaf, in his book *Servant Leadership* (1991), tells us that people will follow leaders who serve them first and then lead them to higher, exciting goals through clear vision and encouragement. Becoming more caring is not something that you wake up on Monday and decide to do. You must practice the habits of caring and kindness over and over until the habit has you. Caring, compassionate leaders seem to love life a little more than do others. They have a good sense of humor and can bring smiles that chase away the hurt and failure in others' lives. Caring leaders, according to Max De Pree (1989), "don't inflict pain; they bear pain" (p. 11). Closely linked to servant leadership is leading with love (Hoyle, 2002a). Leaders must love unconditionally those who are sometimes the most unlovable to turn them into productive team players. When inner love is balanced with love for others, servant leadership becomes a habit. Servant leaders empower others by shining the light on their accomplishments, providing the necessary resources to help all staff members do their jobs, and opening opportunities for growth to all staff members.

Leaders who have developed a capacity for caring hold power over others. A power of admiration and respect and an image of well-being, strength, and energy seem to shine in those who care for others and their welfare. Mehrabian (1971), a behavioral scientist, found that others perceive leaders in three ways. Visual impact constitutes 55 percent of leaders' effect on others, vocal impact is 38 percent, and the words the leaders uses create only 7 percent of the overall impact. Obviously, this researcher found that the way you look and sound in trying to influence others to buy into your vision is far more important than the words you use. Social psychologists tell us that first impressions are the most lasting, which adds validity to the visual impact of 55 percent. However, communications specialists warn of trying to separate the message from the messenger. The bearer of the vision will have far greater success if he or she is viewed as a caring, compassionate person. The way you appear to others has an obvious impact on your ability to lead them to make a vision a reality. If you can clearly articulate the story and concentrate on the why of the vision rather than the how, you will be successful.

Victor Frankl, author of *Man's Search for Meaning* (1967), spent three years as a prisoner in Auschwitz and remained alive under horrible conditions because he knew the "why" of life. He believed that if something in the future was expected (e.g., seeing your child again or finishing a manuscript or project), you could stay alive. He wrote,

> A man who becomes conscious of the responsibility he bears toward a human being who affectionately waits for him, or an unfinished work, will never be able to throw away his life. He knows the "why" for his existence and will be able to bear almost any "how." (p. 127)

A compassionate caring for others is the essence of life and leadership. Author Margaret Wheatley (1992, 2002) believes that if a person sees his or her vocation as a calling, it becomes a spiritual calling to serve others.

LEADERS COMMUNICATE THE VISION CLEARLY

Next, visionary leaders are master communicators, often not for what they say but what they do. Mrs. Shunantona did not tell me how to learn more math the morning I came to her class feeling like a complete failure. She skipped the math sermon and told the class that I was the best first baseman she had ever seen. But I did become a better math student. Dr. Hensarling did not give me a lecture on "quitters never win" or plead with me to stay in the doctoral program to ensure my future. No; he said, "Be better than you think you can be." I took the message to heart and completed my doctorate. Paul Salmon did not tell me that the preparation guidelines were acceptable; he said, "Where are the kids in these guidelines?" The words and the meanings were clear, and they came at a time when I needed to hear them. These leaders knew that "to communicate effectively, the sender's words and symbols must mean the same thing to the receiver that they do to the sender" (Cutlip, Center, & Broom, 1985, p. 261). It takes more than facts to persuade others. Actions sometimes do speak louder than words, and most people would rather see a good example than hear about one.

Our word choice and use are also keys to persuading others. A story out of World War II illustrates the value of clear, carefully chosen words to persuade. Col. David Shoup served as a marine commander in the battle for Tarawa in the South Pacific. Tarawa, said the Japanese, would never be taken by a million men in a hundred years because of the bunkers, pillboxes, and bombproof blockhouses placed there. During an intense firefight to take an airstrip, a young officer ran into Col. Shoup's command post crying that his men couldn't advance because of a machine gun. Disgusted, Shoup responded that it was only one machine gun. The young officer ran back to his men under a hail of gunfire. In a few minutes, he returned to Shoup's command post complaining that there were a thousand marines dug in on the beach and that not one of them would follow him across the airstrip to attack the Japanese. Shoup told him that he had to *ask* who would follow him. He advised that if the officer could get only 10 men to follow him, that 10 was better than none. The young officer clearly got the message and returned for good this time. He led his men to victory and turned the tide of the battle for Tarawa. Clear words filled with emotion and purpose under the most difficult of circumstances moved a thousand marines to win a major battle. Col. David Shoup later became General Shoup, commander of the U.S. Marine Corps. His effective skills in communication helped others see the vision of victory (Leckie, 1978). Captain Sean Sims also had a clear vision of victory and through word and deed communicated that vision of hope to peace-loving people of Iraq. Unfortunately, Sean gave his life to help make that vision happen.

School leaders can improve their visionary skills by developing a stronger vocabulary and becoming more selective of the words they use. The right words will help rally teachers, parents, and community members in establishing local goals and procedures to improve teaching and learning for all students. The skill of clearly communicating student achievement data and the best strategies to align good teaching with good testing is an example of visionary leadership.

A final but equally important communication skill is the art of listening. When you ignore someone talking to you, it is the height of arrogance. It tells the other person that you consider yourself to be superior to him or her. A former sociology professor of mine, Dr. Dan Davis, better known as "Cigar Dan" because of the stub of a cigar permanently positioned in the corner of his mouth, told this story in a lecture about listening to others:

I have seen the horrors of the Nazi concentration camps. Later I worked in Pakistan and witnessed children literally starve to death. But let me tell you something, class, the cruelest form of punishment that one person can inflict upon another is lack of recognition of their existence. If you want to destroy a relationship with another person or close them out of your life forever, stop listening to them.

Good listeners are good communicators. Practice listening to those you love and care about the most, your family, and see if communication improves in your household. Next, practice the listening skills on the job and see the immediate effect on creating shared visions.

LEADERS DON'T GIVE UP

Visionary leaders always finish the race they begin. This commitment to persist separates the successful leaders from the also-rans in learning organizations. Good leadoff hitters are vital to baseball teams, but without the cleanup hitters to drive in the runs, they can't win. Organizations need leaders who can both get on base to start the rally and then drive in the runs as well. Inert ideas abound in all institutions because no individual or group follows up to drive the idea home. Winston Churchill never started a race he didn't finish. Disappointments and failures never doused his fire of persistence.

Three-time Olympic gold medalist Wilma Rudolph never quit anything she started until death took her at age 54. Wilma's race in life got off to a rough start. The 20th of 22 children, Rudolph fought through double pneumonia at age four and then scarlet fever that had her parents thinking she would die. Later, she was stricken with polio, which doctors thought would keep her from walking. With the love and help of her family, who massaged her withered legs, and a cumbersome brace on her left leg, she learned to walk. At age nine, she was required to wear an unattractive high-top shoe. Her burning desire to recover led to the track, where she later inspired the world in the 1960 Olympics in Rome by winning gold medals in the 100- and 200-meter races and the 400-meter relay. Rudolph did not rest on her laurels; she became a successful teacher, businesswoman, coach, and lecturer, and president of the Wilma Rudolph Foundation, which was dedicated to teaching youngsters to overcome obstacles in their lives. After she won the gold medals, the city of Clarksville, Tennessee, wanted to have a victory celebration for her homecoming.

Because her town was segregated at the time, Wilma Rudolph refused to participate in a victory parade unless it was integrated for everyone. With this gesture of love, she brought her hometown together as one people. She was a sharing, caring person who had a vision for her race and for children who needed a boost in life. Tennessee Governor Ned McWhorter eulogized her this way: "Wilma Rudolph's greatest race was not on the field. Her greatest race was won through her experiences throughout her life. The race included many hurdles. She overcame them to become one of the most famous athletes in history." Wilma Rudolph started and finished the race. Her quality of persistence is a model for all of us who attempt to lead others to a better future.

School leaders faced with critical publics, budget cuts, rules, and policies to regulate everything from asbestos to Netscape need all of the Rudolph grit they can muster. New developments in learning technologies and the knowledge society place school principals between superintendents who want better test scores and more National Merit Finalists and parents who demand special programs for "their children." Teachers invariably complain about parents, not about students. Recently, a young first-grade teacher told me, "If it were not for the irrational parents, my job would be wonderful." Parents are worried about the future and how their children will survive without the best education, and they turn their anxiety toward educators, who perceive it to be criticism. Peter Drucker, in his book *Post-Capitalist Society* (1993), heightens the pressures on educators by reminding us that education is the center of the knowledge society, and he challenges educators to help learners center on the most important knowledge and to develop new ways to teach that knowledge. Faced with these and other daunting questions, it is easier to abandon ship and leave the challenges to future generations of educators. Dr. Paul Hensarling's words keep returning to all of his former students who want to drop out of the race. "Be better than you think you can be" strikes at the heart of a true professional who has a vision for better schools and a better society for all people.

Many of the most talented and visionary school leaders I know are tired of the hassles that come with public service in education. They, along with cooperative extension and other human service agency leaders, are taking early retirement. Although this desire for a break from high visibility and pressure is understandable and well earned, I weep for the communities and children who will lose a person at the young age of 55 or 60 with accumulated knowledge that can never be replaced. In fact, recent research by Lydia Bronte (1993) found that more than half of the 150 Americans she interviewed who made significant achievements started their period of peak creativity after age 50. Bronte contends that because people are living longer and have better health at older ages, we have expanded the meaning of middle age. She believes that the new middle age is 50 to 75 years. People this age are healthy and energetic, but they seem to have lost their spark for life or the challenge in their jobs. I ask my middle-aged friends if they have finished the race. My question may be unfair, but it is asked with the best of intentions to persuade a mature leader to reconsider leaving the race so early. He or she has spent a lifetime learning, gaining respect from a wide constituency, and making immeasurable contributions to the community, state, and nation. How about you, the reader of this short book on visionary leadership? Will your vision go unfinished? Will the ideas you have tried to implement lie fallow because you were not there to cultivate them and make them grow into a reality for kids or clients? Finish the race and make your vision become a reality.

A story is told about the world-renowned violinist Fritz Kreisler, who knew the value of persistence in the face of difficulty. After a brilliant performance a lady told Kreisler, "I would give my life to be able to play a violin like that." "Madam," said Kreisler, "I did" (Teaff, 1994). Servant leaders give their lives to a cause greater than themselves; they lead by example, inspire others with their words of encouragement, and work longer and harder to make visions come true.

CONCLUSIONS

To become the kind of person and visionary leader you wish to be is obviously more complex than following the instructions included in this chapter. Scholars who write about leadership and vision reinforce the connections between the three characteristics of the servant leaders I knew or wish I had known: a capacity for caring for others, communication with clear and visionary ideas, and a commitment to persist. These three characteristics encompass relationships and interactions with others—working with others to get the job done and helping others gain the skills and confidence to pursue a vision of success. They are the skills that were basic to the leadership of

Mrs. Shunantona, Dr. Hensarling, Dr. Salmon, Jesus of Nazareth, Joan of Arc, Winston Churchill, and Sean Sims. Work on improving your skills in these three areas, and watch your servant leadership improve and your influence expand. Visionary leaders can be developed, and the ability to persuade others to join you in the pursuit of your dream can happen. It is up to you.

This book began with a story about Notre Dame football coach Charlie Weis keeping a promise and making a vision happen for a dying 10-year-old boy named Montana. Coach Weis and other leaders who serve others, communicate that service through words and deeds, and finish what they start are visionary leaders of the highest level. What about you? How will you finish your vision?

I will close this book with a story about a beautiful 10-year-old red-headed girl named Emma. Two years ago I ran in a 5K race to raise funds to fight Parkinson's disease, a disease that had killed my friend Tom Chandler, a legendary head baseball coach at Texas A&M University. While running in a drizzling rain, I looked back and saw that little Emma was catching me from behind. I asked her to run with me and told her that if she would finish the race I would also. After 30 minutes of plodding along, I was considerably ahead of Emma and decided to finish strong the last three hundred yards. I began to hear cheering from the crowd and got the false impression the cheers were for me—the old guy! They weren't. They were for Emma with her head back, red hair flying in the wind, trying to catch me. I was impressed with her no-quit attitude and decided to step back and let her finish in front of me. She kept her end of our deal and I honored her commitment. When I see Emma at church on Sunday I ask about her schoolwork and especially about her track successes. In both areas Emma will finish strong.

Bibliography and References

Annotated Bibliography

Bolman, L., & Deal, T. (2003). *Reframing the path to school leadership.* Thousand Oaks, CA: Corwin Press.

A well-written, practical look at real-world leadership through the use of dialogue between administrators and staff.

Chance, E. (1992). *Visionary leadership in schools.* Springfield, IL: Charles C Thomas.

Strategies to assist school leaders in developing shared visions for school improvement, including several helpful workshop activities for facilitating the visioning process.

Cornish, E. (2004). *Futuring: The exploration of the future.* Bethesda, MD: World Future Society.

Written for beginning and veteran futurists, this book gives readers a basic knowledge of futuring and how to think about the future. Cornish warns that we cannot make wise decisions if we do not know world trends and their likely consequences. He explores six supertrends of the future, futuring methods, the use of scenarios, and understanding change with fresh, new approaches.

Covey, S. (1990). *Principle-centered leadership.* New York: Simon & Schuster.

Incorporates the seven habits of highly effective people into this classic work. Principle-centered leaders work with competence on the basis of natural principles and build those principles into the center or moral compass of their lives.

Didsbury, H. F., Jr. (2003). *21st century opportunities and challenges.* Bethesda, MD: World Future Society.

An excellent book on advanced technologies and their impact on the future. Its chapters on assessing scientific and technological innovations are excellent for researchers and students.

Drucker, P. (1993). *Post-capitalist society.* New York: Harper.

An exceptional description of social transformations in the twentieth century with special emphasis on knowledge workers, who will give the emerging knowledge society its character and its leadership. Drucker proclaims that education will become the center of the knowledge society and that specialized knowledge will be the key to visionary leadership.

Friedman, T. L. (2005). *The world is flat.* New York: Farrar, Straus and Giroux.

How to translate complex foreign policy and economic issues in the flattened world of the twenty-first century. An excellent read on the world's changing dynamics and what these changes mean for America. You need to read this book.

Hoyle, J. (2002). *Leadership and the force of love: Six keys to motivating with love.* Thousand Oaks, CA: Corwin Press.

For planning the future, no power is as great as love in making visions come true. Examines leading with love in visioning, communicating, mentoring, team-working, empowering, and evaluating. If you can't love, you can't lead.

Hoyle, J., English, F., & Steffy, B. (1998). *Skills for successful 21st century school leaders.* Lancaster, PA: Scarecrow Press.

Presents nine knowledge/skill areas that provide the foundation for the field of educational administration. Includes self-help checklists to assist professors and students in improving their visionary leadership. The only resource that combines national standards created by the American Association of School Administrators, the National Council for the Accreditation of Colleges of Education, and the Interstate School Leaders Licensure Consortium, it is widely used in leadership preparation programs and in preparing for state superintendent and principal licensure exams.

Kennedy, P. (1993). *Preparing for the 21st century.* New York: Random House.

A comprehensive look at global population projections, technological advances, food and fiber production and distribution, communications, conflict, and community development.

Kouzes, J., & Posner, B. (1987). *The leadership challenge.* San Francisco: Jossey-Bass.

A clear, practical description of leaders at their best. Designed to help the reader gain skills in inspiring a shared vision and in attracting people to common purposes.

Russell, C. (1993). *The master trend: How the baby boom generation is remaking America.* New York: Plenum.

A look at the impact of baby boomers and their offspring on the future of America. Issues of education, the labor market, families, health care, and retirement challenge the thinking of leaders in education and other human service agencies.

References

Amundson, K. (1988). *Challenges for school leaders.* Arlington, VA: American Association of School Administrators.
Banfield, S. (1985). *Joan of Arc.* New York: Chelsea House.
Barker, J. (1991). *The power of vision* [video]. (Available from Star Thrower Products, http://www.starthrower.com)
Bartos, O., & Hanson, R. (1976). Constructing simple theories from propositional inventories. *Social Science Research, 5,* 279–314.
Bennis, W., & Nanus, B. (1985). *Leaders: The strategies for taking charge.* New York: Harper & Row.
Berry, L. (1995). *On great service: A framework for action.* New York: Free Press.
Bishop, P. (1994, December). Directory and lecture notes. Project 2020 Vision Workshop, Dallas, TX.
Blanchard, K. (2002). *Whale done.* New York: Free Press.
Bronte, L. (1993). *The longevity factor.* New York: HarperCollins.
Brooks, P. (1954). The greatest life ever lived. In W. B. Gamble (Ed.), *"Well said!" Benedicte's scrapbook: A treasury of illustrations for pastors, teachers, Christian workers, and other public speakers* (p. 2). Grand Rapids, MI: Eerdmans.
Buckingham, M., & Coffman, C. (1999). *First, break all the rules.* New York: Free Press.
Burns, J. (1978). *Leadership.* New York: Harper & Row.
Burton, L. (2003). Convergence and collision: Assessing the impacts of emerging scientific and technological innovations by using applied

foresight. In H. Didsbury (Ed.), *21st century opportunities and challenges* (pp. 3–7). Bethesda, MD: World Future Society.

Chopra, D. (2002). The soul of leadership. *The School Administrator, 8*(59), 10–14.

Conger, J. (1989). *The charismatic leader.* San Francisco: Jossey-Bass.

Cornish, E. (2004). *Futuring: The exploration of the future.* Bethesda, MD: World Future Society.

Covey, S. R. (1990). *Principle-centered leadership.* New York: Simon & Schuster.

Crow, G., Matthews, J., & McCleary, L. (1996). *Leadership.* Larchmont, NY: Eye on Education Press.

Cunningham, W. G. (1982). *Systematic planning for educational change.* Palo Alto, CA: Mayfield.

Cunningham, W., & Cordeiro, P. (2005). *Educational leadership: A problem-based approach* (3rd ed.). Boston: Allyn & Bacon.

Cutlip, S. M., Center, A. H., & Broom, G. M. (1985). *Effective public relations* (6th ed.). Englewood Cliffs, NJ: Prentice Hall.

De Pree, M. (1989). *Leadership is an art.* New York: Dell.

DeCharms, R. (1984). Motivating enhancement in educational settings. In R. Ames & C. Ames (Eds.), *Research on motivation in education: Vol. 1. Student motivation* (pp. 275–310). New York: Academic Press.

Deming, E. (1982). *Out of the crisis: Quality, productivity, and competitive position.* New York: Cambridge University Press.

Deming, E. (1993). *The new economics for industry, government, and education.* Cambridge: MIT, Center for Engineering Study.

Drain, T. (1998, December). *Reform trends facing athletic programs in the 21st century as identified by Division I athletic directors.* Unpublished doctoral dissertation, Texas A&M University, College Station.

Drucker, P. (1993). *Post-capitalist society.* New York: Harper.

Drucker, P. (1994). The age of social transformation. *The Atlantic Monthly,* November, 53–80.

Frankl, V. (1967). *Man's search for meaning.* New York: Washington Square.

Friedman, T. L. (2005). *The world is flat.* New York: Farrar, Straus and Giroux.

Fullen, M. (2003). *The moral imperative of school leadership.* Thousand Oaks, CA: Corwin Press.

Getzels, J., & Guba, E. (1957). Social behavior and the administrative process. *The School Review 65*(4), 423–441.

Glickman, C. D. (1993). *Renewing America's schools: A guide for school-based action.* San Francisco: Jossey-Bass.

Greenleaf, R. K. (1991). *Servant leadership: A journey into the nature of legitimate power and greatness.* Mahwah, NJ: Paulist.

Herzberg, F. (1968, January-February). One more time: How do you motivate employees? *Harvard Business Review, 46*(1), 53–62.

Hoy, W., & Miskel, W. (2005). *Educational administration.* Boston: McGraw-Hill.

Hoyle, J. (1995). A vision of the future and the new school principal. In M. Richardson, M. Flanagan, & K. Lane (Eds.), *School empowerment* (pp. 215–227). Lancaster, PA: Technomic.

Hoyle, J. (2002a). *Leadership and the force of love: Six keys to motivating with love.* Thousand Oaks, CA: Corwin Press.

Hoyle, J. (2002b). The highest form of leadership. *The School Administrator, 8*(59), 18–22.

Hoyle, J., Bjork, L., Collier, V., & Glass, T. (2005). *The superintendent as CEO: Standards based performance.* Thousand Oaks, CA: Corwin Press.

Hoyle, J., & Collier, V. (2005). Systems leadership in reducing school dropouts. *Insight, 20*(2), 16–19.

Hoyle, J., English, F., & Steffy, B. (1985). *Skills for successful school leaders.* Arlington, VA: American Association of School Administrators.

Hoyle, J., English, F., & Steffy, B. (1998). *Skills for successful 21st century school leaders.* Lancaster, PA: Scarecrow Press.

Huffman, H. (2004, November 28). He was willing to make that sacrifice [Electronic version]. *The Bryan–College Station Eagle.* Retrieved October 5, 2005, from http://www.theeagle.com/aandmnews/112804 .Sims.php

Hull, C. (1943). *Principles of behavior.* New York: Appleton-Century-Crofts.

Johnson, S. (1998). *Who moved my cheese?* New York: Putnam.

Kahn, H. (1960). *On thermonuclear war.* Princeton, NJ: Princeton University Press.

Kahn, H. (1982). *The coming boom: Economic, political, and social.* New York: Simon & Schuster.

Kahn, H., Brown, W., & Martel, L. (1976). *The next 200 years: A scenario for America and the world.* New York: Morrow.

Kanter, R. (1983). *The change masters: Innovation and entrepreneurship in the American corporation.* New York: Simon & Schuster.

Kennedy, P. (1993). *Preparing for the 21st century.* New York: Random House.

Kouzes, J., & Posner, B. (1987). *The leadership challenge.* San Francisco: Jossey-Bass.

Leckie, R. (1978). Tarawa: Conquest of the unconquerable. In *Readers digest illustrated stories of World War II* (pp. 236–249). Pleasantville, NY: Readers Digest Association.

Lewin, K. (1948). The consequences of an authoritarian and democratic leadership. In G. Weiss (Ed.), *Resolving social conflicts* (pp. 25–36). New York: Harper & Row.

Locke, E. A., & Latham, G. P. (1990). *A theory of goal setting and task performance.* Englewood Cliffs, NJ: Prentice Hall.

Machiavelli, N. (1992). *The prince.* New York: Dover. (Original work published 1532)

Manchester, W. (1983). *The last lion: Winston Spencer Churchill: Visions of glory, 1874–1932.* Boston: Little, Brown.

Manners, G. E., & Steger, J. A. (1979). The implications of research on the R&D manager's role in the selection and training of scientists and engineers for management. *R&D Management, 9,* 85–92.

Martin, G. (2005). How to stop dealing with the same types of problems day after day, Part 2. *AASA Journal of Scholarship and Practice,* Spring, 18–23.

Maslow, A. (1954). *Motivation and personality.* New York: Harper & Row.

McClelland, D. (1978). The two faces of power. In D. Hampton, C. Sumner, & R. Webber (Eds.), *Organizational behavior and practices of management* (p. 30). Glenview, IL: Scott Foresman.

McGregor, D. (1985). *The human side of enterprise* (25th anniversary printing). New York: McGraw-Hill.

Mehrabian, A. (1971). *Silent messages.* Belmont, CA: Wadsworth.

Montgomery, R. (1997). Collaborative planning for the 21st century: Theory meets practice at the grassroots. In L. Wildman School administration (Eds.), *The new knowledge base* (pp. 304–314). Lancaster, PA: Technomic.

Owens, R. (2000). *Organizational behavior in education.* Boston: Allyn & Bacon.

Popham, J. (2003). Trouble with testing: Why standards-based assessment doesn't measure up. *American School Board Journal, 190*(2), 3–8.

Population Reference Bureau. (2006). *The World's Youth 2006 Data Sheet.* Retrieved February 22, 2006, from http://www.prb.org

Rebore, R. W. (2003). *Personnel administration in education* (3rd ed.). Englewood Cliffs, NJ: Prentice Hall.

Riley, P. (1993). *The winner within.* New York: Putnam.

Rogers, E. M. (1985). Methodology for meta-research. In H. H. Greenbaum, S. A. Helweg, & J. W. Walter (Eds.), *Organizational communications: Abstracts, analysis and overview* (Vol. 10, pp. 12–24). Beverly Hills, CA: Sage.

Rogers, J. (1986). *Winston Churchill.* New York: Chelsea House.

Rowan, R. (1986). *The intuitive manager.* New York: Berkeley Books.

Scruggs, J. C., & Swerdlow, J. L. (1985). *To heal a nation.* New York: Harper & Row.

Senge, P. (1990). *The fifth discipline.* New York: Doubleday.

Senge, P., Cambron-McCabe, N., Lucas, T., Smith, B., Dutton, J., & Kleiner, A. (2000). *Schools that learn.* New York: Doubleday.

Sergiovanni, T. (1992). *Moral leadership: Getting to the heart of school improvement.* San Francisco: Jossey-Bass.

Seymour, P. (1979). *Moments bright and shining.* Norwalk, CT: C. R. Gibson.

Simmons, J. (2005). High performing schools. *Education Week, 25*(9), 46–47, 56.

Skinner, B. F. (1974). *About behaviorism.* New York: Knopf.

Stipek, D. (1996). Motivation and instruction. In D. Berliner & R. Chaffee (Eds.), *Handbook of educational psychology* (pp. 85–113). New York: Macmillan.

Stogdill, R. (1981). Traits of leadership: A follow-up to 1970. In B. Bass (Ed.), *Stogdill's handbook of leadership* (pp. 73–97). New York: Free Press.

Taylor, F. (1947). *Scientific management.* New York: Harper & Row.

Teaff, G. (1994). *Coaching in the classroom.* Waco, TX: Cord Communications.

Thorndike, E. (1911). *Animal intelligence.* New York: Macmillan.

Tillman, L., Lopez, G., Larson, C., Capper, C., Scheurich, J., & Marshall, C. (2003). Leadership in social justice: Identifying the terrain, crafting a mission and purpose. In F. Lunenbert & C. Carr (Eds.), *Shaping the future: NCPEA Yearbook* (pp. 85–98). Lanham, MD: Scarecrow Press.

Tough, A. (2003). Four urgent requests from future generations. In H. Didsbury (Ed.), *21st century opportunities and challenges* (pp. 126–133). Bethesda, MD: World Future Society.

Vance, M., & Deacon, D. (1995). *Think out of the box.* Franklin Lakes, NJ: Career Press.

Wheatley, M. (1992). *Leadership and the new science.* San Francisco: Berrett-Koehler.

Wheatley, M. (2002). Spirituality in turbulent times. *The School Administrator, 8,* 59.

Index

Administrators, school 17,
    19, 42, 44, 67
American Association of School
    Administrators (AASA),
    42–44
Authoritarian leaders, 16–17

Backcasting, 90–91
Barker, J., 101–102
Barker, J., 7
Belief statements, 30–31, 83–85
Beliefs, convictions, visions,
    actions workshop, 77–84
Bennis, W., 2, 10
Berry, L., 100–101
Bezold, C., 30
Bishop, P., 77
Blanchard, K., 14
Blum, A., 102
Bronte, L., 108
Brooks, P., 47
Broom, G., 61
Buckingham, M., 59–60
Burns, J. M. B., 18
Burton, L., 12

Caring leaders, 102–104
Center, A., 61
Champlain, J., 66–67
Change, 12–14
Charismatic Leader (Conger), 100
Chopra, D., 22
Churchill, W., 49–51

City leaders, 17
Coffman, C., 59–60
Communication, 104–106
Community involvement, 67–68
Conger, J., 100
Cordeiro, P., 34
Cornish, E., 24, 26, 86
Covey, S., 75–76
Crow, G., 15
Cunningham, W. G., 34, 93–94
Cutlip, S., 61

Davis, D., 105–106
De Pree, M., 21, 99, 103
Deal, T., 20
DeCharms, R., 57
Delphi technique, 92–94
Deming, E., 21
Demographics, 24
Disraeli, B., 99
Drain, T., 94
Drucker, P., 70, 75, 107

Edison Schools, 60
Educators, visionary, 37–46,
    66–67, 70–72, 78–79, 99

Fifth Discipline (Senge),
    68–69
Frankl, V., 103–104
Friedman, T., 2, 79
Fuller, M., 29
Funding, 69–70

Future society propositions
    workshop, 87–90
Future studies, 24, 26
Futuring, 3, 24–29, 63
*Futuring: The Exploration of
    the Future* (Cornish), 86
The Futurist Magazine, 87
Futurists, 7, 24–27, 60

Gandhi, M., 10
Gates, B., 29
General Electric, 69
Getzels-Guba model, 18
Goal statements, 32–33
Goal theory, 57
Goals, instructional, 32–33
Greenleaf, R. K., 103
Group exercises. *See* Workshops
Group vision, 68–70, 76
Gulf Coast Consortium Tech Prep
    Conference, 94–97

Hawking, S., 10
Hensarling, P. R., 40–42
Herzberg, F., 59
High achievers, 101
Hull, C., 56
Huntsville (TX) Independent
    School District, 78–85

Imagineering, 2
Institute for Alternative
    Futures, 30
Institute for Futures Research, 77
Instructional goals, 32–33
Interstate School Leaders
    Licensure Consortium
    (ISLLC), 44

Jesus of Nazareth, 47–48
Joan of Arc, 48–49
Johnson City (NY) schools, 66–67
Johnson, S., 13

Kahn, H., 90
Kanter, R. B., 20
Kennedy, J. F., Jr., 29, 60
Kidder, R., 30
Kinney, S., 70
Kissinger, H., 2
Kreisler, F., 108

Latham, G. P., 57
Lavington, C., 102
Leaders
    authoritarian, 16–17
    caring, 102–104
    city, 17
    corporate, 69
    participatory, 19–20
    school, 40–46, 66–67. *See also*
        School leadership
    transactional, 18–19
    transformational, 20–23
Leadership
    categories, 15–16
    communication and, 104–106
    effective, 9–11, 34, 45–46
    ethical and moral, 11, 21
    scenarios, 35–36
    school. *See* School leadership
    spiritual, 22
    style, 11, 23, 33–34
*Leadership and the New
    Science (*Wheatley), 97
Lewin, K.,13
Likelihood of Occurrence
    exercise, 87–88
Locke, E. A., 57
Love, leading with, 21–22

Machiavelli, N., 16
Mackey, W., 71–72
Man's Search for Meaning
    (Frankl), 103–104
Manners, G., 61
Martin, G., 11

Maslow, A., 57
Matthews, J., 15
McCleary, L., 15
McClelland, D., 101
McGregor, D., 16
Mehrabian, A., 103
Mission statements, 31–32, 83–85.
    See also Vision statements
Money, 69–70
Montgomery, R., 78–79
Moral leadership, 11, 21
Mother Teresa, 10
Motivation, 56–60
Mussolini, B., 16

Nanus, B., 2, 10
National Council for the
    Accreditation of Colleges
    of Education (NCATE), 44
No Child Left Behind Act,
    4, 17, 32
Nominal Group Process, 81

Occurrence likelihood exercise,
    87–88
Organizations
  belief statements of, 30
  change in 13, 69, 70
  learning, 69
  service vision of, 99–102
  team-building in, 70
  transactional leadership in,
      18–20
  transformation of, 2–3, 10–11
Owens, R., 18

Parks, R., 29
Participative leaders, 19–20
Personal vision workshop, 76–77
Persuasion, 61–63
Poor children, 27, 35
Post-Capitalist Society
    (Drucker), 107

Power of Vision (Lavington),
    101–102
The Prince (Machiavelli), 16
Principals, 19, 43

Riley, P., 99
Risk taking, 68–69, 71
Rudolph, W., 106–107

Salmon, P. B., 42–44
Sanders, D., 95–96
Scenarios, 90–92
Schlesinger, A. M., Jr., 53
School administrators, 17, 19, 42,
    44, 67
School boards, 19, 20, 66
School districts, 14–15, 20, 29–31,
    72, 77–85
School Empowerment
    (Richardson), 87
School leaders, visionary, 40–46,
    66–67
School leadership
  authoritarian, 17,
  change in, 22–23
  ethical and moral, 11, 21
  participative, 20,
  social justice in, 22
  spiritual, 22
  visionary, 30, 40–46, 66–67
School superintendents, 19, 43,
    71, 78, 89, 99
Schools
  poorly performing, 14–15
  vision in, 69–70. *See also*
      School leadership
Schools for the future workshop,
    86–87
Schools That Learn (Senge), 87
Scruggs, J., 65–66
Senge, P., 29, 68–69, 87
Sergiovanni, T., 20–21
Servant leaders, 102–103

Servant Leadership
    (Greenleaf), 103
Shakespeare, W., 27
Shoup, D., 104–105
Shunantona, B., Mrs., 37–40
Sims, S., 51–53
*Skills for Successful 21st Century
    School Leaders* (Hoyle),
    43–44
Skinner, B. F., 56
Smith, H. B., 55–56
Social justice, 22
Spiritual leadership, 22
Staff development. *See* Workshops
Steger, J., 61
Stengel, C., 75
Superintendents, 19, 43, 71, 78,
    89, 99
*Systematic Planning for
    Educational Change*
    (Cunningham), 94

Taylor, F., 16
Teaff, G., 34, 57–58
Tech prep education, 94–96
Technology, 79, 95–97
Theory X, 16
Think Out of the Box (Vance), 1
Thorndike, E., 56
Tillman, L., 21
Tough, A., 27
Transactional leaders, 18–19
Transformational leaders, 20–23

Vietnam Memorial Fund, 66
Vision
    definition of, 30
    implementing, 67–73, 78–84

in organizations, 7
in schools, 69–70. *See also*
    School leadership
shared, 68–70, 76
Vision statements, 29–30. *See also*
    Mission statements
Visionaries, 2, 100. *See also*
    Visionary leaders
Visionary educators, 37–44,
    66–67, 70–72, 78–79, 99
Visionary leaders
    characteristics of, 100–101
    examples of, 37–53,
    motivating others, 59–60
    motivation of, 56–57
    persistence of, 106
    strategies of, 60, 68
Visioning. *See* Futuring

Weis, C., 8–9
Welch, J., 69
Wells, H. G., 29
Whale Done (Blanchard), 14
Wheatley, M. J., 97
Who Moved My Cheese?
    (Johnson), 13
Workshops
    beliefs, convictions, visions,
        actions, 77–84
    Delphi technique, 92–94
    future society propositions,
        87–90
    personal vision, 76–77
    schools for the future, 86–87
World Future Society,
    24, 28, 87
The World Is Flat
    (Friedman), 79